The Road to the Super Bowl

by Bob Ryan

A Division of Howard W. Sams & Company

Published by Masters Press
A Division of Howard W. Sams & Company
2647 Waterfront Pkwy E. Dr, Suite 100
Indianapolis, IN 46214

97 98 99 00 01 02   10 9 8 7 6 5 4 3 2 1

Library of Congress
Cataloging in Publication Information

Ryan, Bob, 1946-
    The road to the Super Bowl / by Bob Ryan.
        p. cm.
    ISBN 1-57028-136-X
    1. New England Patriots (Football team) 2. Super
Bowl (Football game) I. Title.

GV956.N36R93   1997
796.332'64'09744--dc21   97-10425
                                              CIP

Dedication

To Keith and Jessica:
How is it possible you two sprang
from the same womb?

Credits

Cover Photos©James W. Biever (front) and Tom Miller (back)

Inside Photos©Tom Miller and James W. Biever

Edited by Kim Heusel

Cover Design by Phil Velikan

Text Layout by Kim Heusel

Table of Contents

Introduction

Credibility.

If you were the 1993 New England Patriots, and you were 9-39 in the three previous years, and your season ticket fan base had shrunk to 18,000 or so fans, and you were perhaps the only franchise in the National Football League fourth out of four teams in terms of local interest and prestige and you were in truly desperate need of a move that would give you instant credibility, you would probably do what Patriots owner James Busch Orthwein did on January 21, 1993.

You would open your checkbook and you would throw money at Duane Charles (Bill) Parcells. You would convince him that it was time to end his two-year self- and health-imposed exile from the coaching ranks. You would tell him that it was time for him to stop masquerading as an NBA and MSG television analyst and go back to doing what he did better than anyone in the world. You would give him control of your football team.

In time, people would forget the contribution Budweiser heir James Busch Orthwein made to the New England Patriots. He often looked and acted like a Mel Brooks vision of an NFL owner, but history will show that he performed an enormous service to the franchise after assuming control in the wake of Victor Kiam's disastrous stewardship. He kept the team in Boston, he hired Bill Parcells and then he sold the team to a local man, Robert Kraft. Few in Boston have ever said thanks.

The New England (nee Boston) Patriots had come into being on November 18, 1959, when William H. (Billy) Sullivan came up with $25,000 to secure the eighth and final spot in the new American Football League. Five months later the team had a name: the Patriots. The new team would play its home games at Braves Field, which had last housed a professional sports team eight years earlier, when the Boston Braves had played their last National League schedule before skipping off to Milwaukee just prior to the 1953 season. It would be the first of five home sites for the team, not including the official "home" game the team once played in Birmingham, Alabama.

Billy Sullivan was known to everyone in Boston who followed sports. He had been the sports information director at Boston College (his alma mater) under Frank Leahy. He had been the publicity director of the Boston Braves during the pennant season of 1948. He had been in on the ground floor of the Jimmy Fund, the nickname for the charity which funds research and treatment for children's cancer. He had been in the movie business in Hollywood during the '50s. He was in the heating oil business. He was an all-around sports gadfly. He could be charming and boorish — in the same sentence. For the next 29 years he would hold onto the franchise.

When the time came to sell, Billy Sullivan was left with few good choices. He sold the club to Victor Kiam, a man who had the bore part down without ever getting a handle on the charm part. He was well known because he was the owner of the Remington Razor Company. He became a quasi-celebrity by doing his own commercials, and was known for saying how he had come to appreciate the product so much that he bought the company. Too bad he couldn't have purchased a personality and some common sports sense with his money.

He wound up selling the team to James Busch Orthwein, whose apparent intention when he gained control was to use it as a negotiating tool with the National Football League in his quest to get an expansion franchise for his beloved home city of St. Louis. He hired the management/coaching duo of Sam Jankovitz and Dick McPherson to run his team, and the immediate result was a 6-10 record in 1991, which represented a definite improvement over the Rod Rust-coached 1-15 team a year earlier.

Orthwein had always scared people, but in the end he treated the franchise with fairness and kindness. He signed Parcells, kept the team one more year and then sold it on January 21, 1994, to Robert Kraft, a 52-year-old businessman who then had control of Foxboro Stadium and who had then been the owner of six season tickets purchased in 1971, the first year the team had played in the first stadium it ever had to call its very own.

Whereas Orthwein had been a benign, hands-off and largely unseen presence who had allowed Parcells to do whatever he wished in terms of personnel procurement, Kraft would prove to be more the scrutinizing sort. In time, his management style and his personality would conflict with the Parcells ego and the Parcells self-image. In the end the two would wind up like litigants in a bitter mutual divorce. But before the partnership would dissolve in bitter and phenomenally public fashion in late January and early February of 1997, the two would preside over the happiest days in the history of a very beleaguered franchise. With Bob Kraft owning and prodding and probing and questioning and just plain nudging; and with Bill Parcells utilizing coaching and motivational skills bequeathed to a select few, the Patriots would rise from a 2-14 launching pad in the last pre-Parcells year to an American Football Conference championship and a berth in Super Bowl XXXI, where they would engage the mighty Green Bay Packers in a legitimate battle of football equals.

And then Bill Parcells, his mind locked onto a return to his home state of New Jersey and his wallet newly stuffed with many Alexander Hamiltons, courtesy of octogenarian oil magnate Leon Hess, would exit acrimoniously, his dream of bringing a world's championship to New England unfulfilled. But he would leave the New England Patriots in far better shape than he found them. He would leave his successor, Pete Carroll, in possession of a fine collection of young talent. He would leave his owner with a long waiting list for season tickets. He would leave the generic New England sports fan panting for the arrival of a new football season, and that is something that had never happened before.

Bill Parcells had presided over the development of young stars such as quarterback Drew Bledsoe, whom he had selected out of Washington State University to be the cornerstone of the franchise when he had the first draft pick in the country; Ben Coates, an unheralded fifth-round draft pick out of tiny Livingston College who would become, under Parcells, one of the great tight ends in the game; Willie McGinest, a linebacker-turned-defensive end out of the University of Southern California whom Parcells would develop into a superb pass rusher and game breaker; and Curtis Martin, a quiet, religious, humble and phenomenally talented running back out of Pittsburgh who would gain more than 1,000 yards in each of his first two seasons in the league.

Bill Parcells took the New England Patriots from the middle pages and made them sports conversation Topic A in the middle of a baseball pennant race. Bill Parcells, by virtue of just being himself, evolved into the single biggest sports personality in Boston. When he finally left town, he was substantially bigger than any player.

Everyone knew him as The Tuna, and even that nickname had its own conflicting mythology. He said it came about in 1980, when the Starkist Tuna people had an ad campaign featuring a know-it-all tuna named Charlie. He says it evolved from a situation in which he said, "You think I'm Charlie the Tuna?" or some such thing. Funny. Most people took one look at him, tumbling out of his sweatshirt, and assumed he was nicknamed Tuna because he sure as hell was built like one. But The Tuna had his story, and he was sticking to it. Which is exactly what everyone expected from Bill Parcells, aka The Tuna.

He was a master media manipulator. He controlled the entire agenda, but he was able to get away with it because 10 minutes with him was better than two hours with most coaches. He could be informative, witty, caustic, charming and insulting in a five-minute span. He was completely autocratic. He forbid his assistants from speaking to the press, a preposterous pretention, and he got away with it. He learned about the foibles and interests of individual members of the press, and he knew how to use his information to his advantage.

He was a writer's dream. During the 1996-97 Super Bowl run, he was the O.J. to many journalists' Geraldo. His daily chats, better known as Tuna Talks, were often virtuoso performances. Had they all been collected on tape, they would have provided a stunning football education. He thought he was smarter than everyone else, and he was usually correct.

The Patriots had made progress in years 1 and 2, going from 6-10 to 10-6, but his team had encountered many different problems in 1995, when Bledsoe sustained a serious shoulder injury in the third game of the season. Nothing ever really went right after that, aside from the spectacular running of Martin, whose 1,487 yards propelled him to AFC Offensive Rookie of the Year honors. Bill Parcells was displeased with a lot of things at the end of 1995-96. Most of all, he was displeased with himself.

There are always things outside anyone's control in sports, be it coach or player. But one thing Bill Parcells knew he could control as the 1996-97 season began was his own effort and preparation. He believed he had not coached like Bill Parcells in 1995. He was determined the world would see the *real* Bill Parcells in 1996-97.

The Exhibition Season

How did they know?

Well, they didn't, of course. No one knew that the first exhibition game of the 1996 preseason for both the New England Patriots and the Green Bay Packers would be the first half of a season's pair of bookends. No one knew that the teams meeting on Friday, August 2, at Green Bay's historic Lambeau Field would be the very teams who would bring a conclusion to the season 25 weeks later in New Orleans. No one knew, but everyone was free to hope.

One of these teams was indeed harboring legitimate Super Bowl hopes, but it certainly wasn't the visiting Patriots. Green Bay simply believed this was going to be its year. The Packers had been making a steady upward climb to the Super Bowl, knocking on the NFC championship door for the better part of three years. The Packers felt they had been paying all the appropriate dues. Their only problem, aside from a degree of uncertainty about the physical status of star quarterback Brett Favre following a well-publicized off-season rehab stay to help kick an addiction to painkillers, was an inability to defeat the hated Dallas Cowboys in Dallas. But the Packers reasoned there was a very easy way around that particular problem. Win enough games during the regular season so there would be no NFC title game in Texas Stadium; that's all. Win enough games to make sure that the NFC title game would be played on what was erroneously, but lovingly, known as the "frozen tundra of Lambeau Field."

The New England Patriots had no such lofty ambitions. The New England Patriots would admit only to wanting a return to the playoffs following a very disappointing 1995 season. Whatever their private personal thoughts, the Patriots kept the serious bravado locked inside.

The coach was happy with the identity of the first exhibition opponent. He had put the squad through a very rugged preseason. It was, according to insiders, a cross between basic training at Parris Island and a re-enactment of *Beau Geste*. Mirth and frivolity were noticeably absent as the Patriots slogged through some miserable days at Bryant College.

Bill Parcells did not like the way his team had performed during the 1995 preseason, and he was going to insure there would be a different attitude this time. He referred to it as "a camp like 1985 — a *Giants* camp." And everyone knew what had taken place at the end of the 1985 season. The New York Giants had gone to the 1986 Super Bowl. Final score: New York 39, Denver 20.

So playing as formidable an opponent as the Green Bay Packers was quite all right with The Tuna. He wanted to see if his tough training camp would be paying any early dividends. "I very much like to play the Green Bay

Packers," Parcells said. "Lambeau Field's a wonderful place to play. The stadium's been redone, the game's a sellout, it's almost like a regular-season environment. And I think it's good for the team."

Parcells went on to say that an ideal first exhibition game "would be if we win, 35-0, and there are no injuries." That bit of semi-levity aside, The Tuna again turned serious. "We didn't play too well in the preseason last year," he said, "and there was a carryover right into the regular season. Some of the problems we had in the preseason games manifested themselves in the regular season."

Away from the field, everything was said to be just hunky-dory between the feisty coach and the fidgety owner. Bob Kraft was especially anxious to put a happy public face on the owner-coach relationship. The storm clouds had already been brewing, dating back to Draft Day, when Kraft had sided with Player Personnel Director Bobby Grier against his coach on the subject of the first pick. Parcells wanted defensive help, but the owner reasoned that he had invested some $42 million in a quarterback, and the QB needed someone to throw to. No one then knew the depth of the rift between the two. All the outside world knew was that Bill Parcells had been signed by James Busch Orthwein with the understanding that he would have the final say on all personnel matters, that he no longer had that authority and that he was, at the very least, agitated.

Kraft went out of his way to play down The Troubles. "You can see how Bill and I interact on the field," said Kraft, referring to public chats back at the Rhode Island practice field. "Everything's fine. We're in this together. The goal of all of us is to make the team better. Bill and I are getting along fine."

The Patriots' first unit seemed to get along fine against Green Bay. When both teams had their primary offensive and defensive units on the field, the Patriots acquitted themselves very well. Drew Bledsoe got off to an 11-for-12 start, the defense shackled Favre (only five completions and no points) and the Patriots led, 7-0. In fact, the postgame talk was so upbeat it was easy to dismiss the fact that the Packers' second and third units had run all over them, and that the home team had actually won the game by a 24-7 score.

But that is the nature of exhibition football. These games are much like the old Hindu tale of the six blind men and the elephant. Each observer can make of the game what he or she wants. Experienced defensive minds could study the Patriots' performance to see how the team reacted to its new 4-3 up-front format, as well as the showing of Willie McGinest, who was playing his first game as right defensive end after spending his first two years in a Patriots uniform as a linebacker. Said McGinest, "I've got a lot to learn. I got a hint of what I have to do and I picked up a lot of stuff I'm going to have to do."

By the end of the season, McGinest had progressed so well he was spending the first Sunday of February in Honolulu as a member of the AFC Pro Bowl team.

Bledsoe watchers, meanwhile, were ecstatic. The 1995 season had been a miserable experience for the kid, who had his shoulder torn apart during the San Francisco game on September 17. It was only the third game of the season, and it set the tone for all sorts of aggravation, physical and otherwise.

One of the interesting additions to the Patriots' cast of characters during the off-season was Chris Palmer, the one-time Boston University mentor and acknowledged offensive expert, who had been brought in as the first quarterback coach of the Parcells era. This was in response to the criticism of many who felt that Bledsoe would benefit from the daily hands-on approach of a soothing voice (in contrast, though few would say so publicly, to Parcells' not-so-dulcet tones).

These Dixville Notch-style returns were very encouraging. Bledsoe was authoritative and crisp, connecting on 11 of 12 pass attempts against a good Green Bay defense for 140 yards, one touchdown and one interception. The touchdown aerial was a 41-yarder to veteran Vincent Brisby who made a fully extended grab of a nice Bledsoe lead. "Hopefully," said Bledsoe, "a lot of things Palmer is teaching will happen this year."

Oh if only the next game had been for real. There are people who have followed the Patriots from Braves Field to Fenway Park to Harvard Stadium to Boston College and through all three names of the current stadium who would gladly have sacrificed the rights to generations yet unborn if only the results up on the Dallas Cowboys' own scoreboard were actually for real. For it was New England 31, Dallas 7, praise the Lord.

The only problem, aside from the obvious: not only was this not a real NFL count-it-in-the-standings game, but this wasn't even a facsimile Dallas team. Among the prominent Cowboys not in uniform were famed running back Emmitt Smith, tight end Jay Novacek, tackle Erik Williams, wide receiver Michael Irvin and center Ray Donaldson. Parcells was so indifferent concerning the outcome that he had nothing whatsoever to say to the media upon the game's conclusion. His only feeling was that it is always better to win than it is to lose. Aside from that, he recognized this game for what it was.

But no one could have been more glum than Dallas coach Barry Switzer. "I'll tell you what I told the team," he said, "and that is, I don't care if this is preseason, but everybody who was part of that game should be embarrassed.'"

Tedy Bruschi, a linebacker out of Arizona, was the perfect Parcells rookie. (Photo©Tom Miller)

Only the young and impressionable among the New England party reveled. "You can say, 'Just an exhibition game,' but it's not," decided second-year cornerback Jimmy Hitchcock. "It's something to build on."

It was undeniably true that the Patriots were feeling good about themselves at this juncture. There was a general, and growing, feeling that this team had more talent than its predecessor, and that its hard work was already paying off. Dave Meggett is anything but impressionable, but he was willing to go public with a very strong statement. "The attitude is a lot different than last year," he said. "At this point we have a much better team."

The new Era of Good Feeling moved right along in the third exhibition game, as the Patriots manhandled a pretty good Philadelphia Eagles team which was attempting to play a very serious game. The score was 37-10, and it was an accurate reflection of the overall New England superiority.

"You guys know me by now," said a dejected Eagles coach Ray Rhodes. "I don't make any excuses. We just had an old-fashioned butt-kicking. We have to go back to the drawing board."

But there were no long faces in the other locker room, where the positive statements started right at the top. "I'm pleased with our progress," said The Tuna. "I want us to be a team that nobody wants to play."

Among the aspects of this convincing triumph which pleased Parcells the most was a strong showing by his special teams and an overall demonstration of team speed. "Yes, we've got more speed," acknowledged Parcells. "We're getting more pressure (on the pass rush), but we'll see when the bullets start flying. We've got better players, but we're not very thick." That was Parcellese for "deep," as in "depth."

With McGinest starting to find himself as a defensive end and pass rusher, the Patriots exerted great pressure on Philadelphia quarterback Rodney Peete, who was sacked three times and finally driven from the game when he found himself the meat of a sandwich in which the bread was supplied by McGinest and feisty, wild-eyed rookie linebacker Tedy Brucshi, a born head-hunter the Patriots had picked up in the third round of the draft.

Bruschi was the perfect Parcells rookie. The Arizona product believed that rookies should be seen and not heard, unless the sound they were making was the re-sounding smack of his helmet separating some poor of-fensive player from the football. "I really don't have much to say to you guys (i.e. the media) now because I want to feel good about myself when it counts" he said after a dazzling performance against the Eagles. "It's just a pre-season game, and when I got in there I did some good things, but I want to do those things in the regular sea-son."

Draftniks were not sure Bruschi could make it in the NFL because of his in-between size (6 feet, 245 pounds), and that was all the motivation Bruschi needed. Bruschi had one more thing to say. "I always try to stay positive about myself," he declared. "I know I can do this and I feel confident about myself and my ability."

Bledsoe threw two more touchdown passes and backup quarterback Scott Zolak led the team to scores on four of his first five drives, but most of the postgame talk centered on the defense. "We're not as big as we were last year up front, but we've got some really good athletes who are quick," said defensive end Mike Jones, who was emerging as a real team leader. "Willie adds so much more speed and pressure to our front, and the four-man front allows our defensive line to get on the corner and get upfield. As far as I'm concerned, the four-man line is easier than the three-man line, where you really had to stay at home. This defense allows us to re-act and get off the ball and be aggressive."

Perhaps a measure of how far the team had come in such a relatively short period of time was just how upset and disgusted (publicly, anyway) Bill Parcells was follow-ing the final exhibition game of the 1996 preseason. "I said before training camp that I want to have a smart team," he said. "This was a dumb team tonight. All of the good things we did were overshadowed by them.

We're not good enough to beat a good opponent if we play like this and make mistakes like we did tonight."

Oh, yeah. The Patriots had just beaten the Washington Redskins by a 27-19 score amid the rain and slop at Foxboro Stadium.

No doubt The Tuna had valid reasons to rant and rave. There were missed assignment and there were penalties. But veteran players knew that the number one goal of the final exhibition game had been accomplished; namely, no one had sustained a major injury. Compared to any other conceivable ramification, nothing else mattered.

"We viewed this as the final exhibition game, and it doesn't mean a thing," said veteran guard William Roberts, an old Parcells mainstay from the glory days in the Meadowlands. "The important thing is that we came out of it healthy and we're ready to step into the regular season."

There was one scare when Bledsoe clutched his left elbow after being sacked by Tony Woods late in the second quarter. He stayed in the game until the third period, when he retired to the sidelines to put an ice bag on the elbow.

The coach, as usual, dismissed the Bledsoe injury as a teeny-tiny owie, and nothing more, a judgment confirmed by the quarterback himself. "It's fine," he smiled. "I just wanted a little sympathy."

Bledsoe might have been fine, but there was one aspect of his game which clearly needed work. It was a problem which began to surface in 1995, and it almost fell into the area of a phobia.

No one had ever had any reason to question his proficiency in the pure area of throwing a football. Drew Bledsoe has as strong an arm as anyone could ask for.

But for some time he had a definite problem throwing the very short pass. Here was a guy who had no difficulty throwing the ball 50 yards upfield, or making that wicked 18-yard sideline toss from the opposite side of the field, but who could not throw a little flare pass. Bledsoe appeared to have a variation of Steve Sax disease. The shorter the pass, the more difficult it was for him to throw.

Given that in Curtis Martin and fullback Sam Gash Bledsoe had been gifted with way above average receivers coming out of the backfield, this was a definite problem. If these passes had to be removed from the Patriots' repertoire because the quarterback couldn't keep a five- or seven-yard toss from bouncing into the ground, it would be utterly ridiculous, not to mention damaging, to the entire offensive scheme.

The coach, who had been watching this go on for more than a half-season, was beginning to lose patience. "He's got to work on his accuracy, particularly on his short passes," said Parcells. "That guy's bending over and he's got to make the American League Play of the Week every time we catch a three-yard pass. We've got to do something about that. He knows that."

It had not been a pleasant week for the coach. Cutdown time for any mentor is a difficult experience, but in his case it was worse than usual because he had been forced to make a very unpleasant decision. He had decided that the best interests of the team lay in keeping one full-time place-kicker, and not two. He had given thought to keeping a kickoff/long field-goal man and a short field-goal man, but he could not justify that kind of luxury in the end. The odd man out was 40-year old Matt Bahr, who was nothing less than one of The Tuna's all-time favorite players.

Given any remote opportunity, Parcells would launch into a detailed analysis of Matt Bahr's career. Parcells believed Bahr was one of the great clutch kickers in NFL history, and he was forever grateful to Bahr for one performance in particular. Bahr had kicked the Giants into the 1991 Super Bowl by kicking five field goals — including the 42-yard game-winner with no time left in a 15-12 victory over San Francisco. Bill Parcells loved Matt Bahr, but rookie Adam Vinatieri had a stronger leg, as Bahr would be the first to concede. Parcells was not entirely comfortable with a rookie kicker, but there was an obvious talent gap in this case, and he decided to go with the kid from South Dakota State and the World League of American Football.

Parcells' end-of-exhibition grousing aside (a coach, after all, is not paid to be a cheerleader or PR man), there was clear reason for optimism as the preseason ended and the regular season beckoned. Anyone watching this team knew it had upgraded its talent level. The improvement in team speed was obvious; Bledsoe was again throwing the ball the way he had in 1994 (4,555 yards, a 58 percent completion percentage and 25 touchdowns); Curtis Martin was clearly every bit as good a running back as he had been in 1995, when he was the AFC Rookie Offensive Player of the Year; and the overall receiving corps had been improved, and this was without even discussing the celebrated first-round pick.

Terry Glenn had not participated in the exhibition games. The fleet wide receiver from Ohio State, whose selection had proven to be an extremely sore spot with the coach, had gotten deep into the Tuna doghouse (the very last bunk in the back of the room) by making the unfortunate mistake of pulling a hamstring. He had also become the very unwilling party of the second part in a training camp *cause celebre*.

Asked one day in a quite innocent manner how the rookie was progressing with his injury, Bill Parcells started

11

out, "Well, *she's*" and he didn't have to go any further. The media mob had its story for the day.

What Parcells was doing was reinforcing the ultra macho man image of the classic football coach. Vince Lombardi had put it in words decades before when he espoused his theory of injury, which went something like this: If you can lie down, you can sit. If you can sit, you can stand. If you can stand, you can walk. If you can walk, you can run. And if you can run, you can play. Suffice it to say that Bill Parcells, like many of his coaching brethren, subscribes wholeheartedly to that entire theory.

Consider that Parcells is wary of rookies in the first place. Then consider that this particular rookie was not merely a rookie, nor merely a number one draft pick. He was a symbol of a deteriorating relationship between the coach and the owner. Bob Kraft might have wanted desperately to convey a joyous partnership front to the world, but those on the inside knew better. Bill Parcells was never going to get over the fact that he didn't have his way on something as crucial to the organization as the first draft pick. This was not the way things were when James Busch Orthwein, and not Bob Kraft, owned the team. And it most assuredly was not the way Bill Parcells wanted it.

All the latent frustration Parcells felt inside leapt out when he uttered the infamous "she" line. In the tight manly world of football, the phrase had only as much meaning as someone wished to attach to it. Terry Glenn was an extremely hard-bitten kid who had been around the block once or twice. To him, it didn't mean a damn thing other than his new coach was irked because the prize property was unavailable for duty. Glenn was bright. He knew all about The Tuna reputation. Glenn couldn't help it if both the press and various women's organizations were going to make a big deal out of this. He just viewed it as a case of someone taking a quarterback sneak and trying to run it 50 yards into the end zone.

Parcells had run a very tough camp and there had been obvious improvement. His desire not to repeat the dull and disastrous 1995 training camp had been fulfilled. The team won three of four games against pretty good opponents. The very idea that his club could make so many mistakes while defeating the Washington Redskins was in itself a very positive sign. Being able to win while giving less than your best effort is a hallmark of good teams in every sport known to man. They can't all be Picassos. Even the Chicago Bulls throw a stinkbomb out there every once in a while.

Bill Parcells had negotiated himself out of the final year of his original five-year contract with the Patriots back in January, but no one on the outside really knew exactly what that meant. Did it mean he was absolutely, positively a lame duck? The only man who possibly knew was Bill Parcells, and he wasn't telling.

What his players knew is that this man was coaching as if he were being paid by the minute. Not to suggest that the 1995 Parcells was slovenly, but even he would admit many times over the course of the coming season that 1995 was not exactly his finest coaching hour. He was never able to reach his team. He would speak of his intense period of self-evaluation, wherein he annually asks himself if he honestly got the best out of his team, and he had no way around the painful conclusion that in 1995 he had not. Oh, Bledsoe had gotten hurt early and had never really recovered, and there were other legitimate talent problems, but Bill Parcells knew what the possibilities had been better than anyone on earth and he believed the 1995 Patriots could have done better than 6-10.

Having cleared his mind of whatever clutter was laying about by eliminating that final season ("I always coach year-to-year, anyway" he would say approximately a thousand times over the next few months), Bill Parcells rededicated himself to being the best coach he could possibly be, and the players had already gotten the message.

"We worked damn hard, but it was good," said Mike Jones. "I can't say I liked going through it, but it brought us together as a team. To go through all that, damn. Now when it's tough we can all think of that and know the only way it was worth is was to win."

Parcells was in a reflective mood as the first game approached. He was even willing to spell out just what it is that keeps bringing him back to the drudgery that is a July-through-December (and, hopefully, beyond) NFL season.

He spoke of what it takes to assemble a team. That's T-E-A-M, team. This isn't golf, and it isn't even baseball, where individual acts layered one on top of another can produce victory. This is football, where guys put their bodies on the line with every play and where the greatest running back who ever lived can do nothing if the line doesn't block (The old New York football Giants once held the legendary Jim Brown to eight yards in seven carries. If that can happen, then anything in football can happen). It's a team game all the way. A quarterback needs someone to catch the ball. An open receiver needs a quarterback to find him. A runner needs a block. A blocker needs a capable runner. The offense needs a defense. The defense needs an offense. Both need the special teams. When it all comes together, a bond is formed which is quite unlike that in any other sport. What gets Bill Parcells off is starting with nothing on the first day of training camp in the hopes that it will all conclude with some thick-necked guy or two dumping Gatorade on him with a minute left in the Super Bowl and his team ahead by 17 points. And what Bill Parcells knows above all else is that only a T-E-A-M can get to that point.

"I realize we got some true mercenaries around the league now who will wear a red shirt for money, or a blue shirt for money," he said. "but that's not me and I hope it's not the players on my team...The whole way the sport is presented now takes away from the team. The sales-manship of the way it's presented is what TV feels is the marquee players, but that's not the way it's ever been in pro football and that's not the way it is today. They just think it is.

"It's not 'Troy Aikman and the Dallas Cowboys,' " he continued. "It's 'The Dallas Cowboys.' Troy Aikman knows that. That's why he's my kind of guy, and I told him that in Dallas. He said he appreciated it. In any suc-cessful organization you've got to get everybody com-mitted to doing the same thing. If an organization does that, you have a chance. If you don't, you cannot win. We have an organization that can win."

Given what would transpire in the last days of Janu-ary, that was a fascinating statement. Bill Parcells would find the whys and wherefores of the New England Patri-ots' organization headed by Bob Kraft unacceptable in January, but that same organization would prove to be manageable in the heat of battle. Who says a great man shouldn't reserve the right to be contradictory?

Among other reasons for local optimism as the regu-lar season began was the Patriots' schedule. Finishing with a 6-10 record the year before had given them a softer 1996 schedule. Now these things have a way of working themselves out in a manner no one could possibly fore-see, but anyone looking at the Patriots' 1996 schedule had to feel comfortable.

The opponents had a combined 1995 winning per-centage of .458. The interconference opponents were coming from the NFC East, which had gone from being the toughest conference in the league in the early '90s to one of the weakest midway through the decade. And whereas in 1995 the Patriots had to play such playoff-bound teams as San Francisco, Kansas City, Pittsburgh and Atlanta — all on the road — this year they would be playing Jacksonville, Baltimore, Denver and San Diego. At the start of the season, the idea of either Denver or Jacksonville being considered among the league's elite was remote.

But so much of a team's success in any sport depends not only on whom you play, but when and where you play them. It was obvious to one and all, for example, that anyone playing Dallas in the first five weeks of the season would be very fortunate. Michael Irvin would be out that long as he served his suspension for being a very naughty boy, and there were other Dallas injuries to be dealt with. This is always the case in any sport.

The Patriots did have one unlucky aspect to their schedule. Their first two games would be on the road. They would be at Miami and at Buffalo. Both teams were divisional rivals, and both figured to be rugged opponents, Miami because it was going to be Jimmy Johnson's very heralded coaching debut, and Buffalo because Buffalo, was, well, Buffalo. It would be very easy for the Patriots to get off to an 0-2 start. An 0-2 start for a veteran-laden team would be one thing, but an 0-2 start for a team so heavily dependent on the fragile psyches of young players would be quite another. It was with a great deal of apprehension that Bill Parcells and his staff approached that opener in Miami.

Game 1

For as long as oranges have fallen off trees in the state of Florida, it seemed that Don Shula had been the coach of the Dolphins. He had become, arguably, the most celebrated man in the entire city. But he just did not know when to get out when the going was good. After years of spinning wheels and teams with no running attacks and shoddy defense, he was eased out by bombastic owner Wayne Huizenga, to be replaced by pro football's resident government in exile.

That would be Jimmy Johnson, who, having left the Dallas Cowboys with two Super Bowl rings, a pile of money and some nasty exit lines from owner Jerry Jones, had taken up residence in south Florida, where he sat on his boat and emerged periodically to steal some easy money as a carefree, what-the-hell TV analyst. He had always made it clear that the coaching job of his dreams

17

would be Miami, and he figured that if he kept his mouth reasonably shut (he did fall off the verbal wagon when he picked the Dolphins to win it all prior to the '95 season, a move interpreted by many as a vicious way to embarrass Shula) and minded his own business, sooner or later Mr. Huizenga would come crawling in his direction, dragging large bags of money behind him.

Few people in the world wanted anything more than Jimmy Johnson wanted to win the first game of the 1996 NFL season. He was at home and he wanted to make a good first impression. True, no one was foolish enough to think that the mere presence of Jimmy Johnson would make the Dolphins a prime contender in the first year, but people thought the team would be respectable at the least and pretty damn good at best. And Jimmy wanted desperately to make a splash in the opener.

There is always reason to fear the Miami Dolphins as long as Dan Marino is there to take the snaps from the center of the moment, and Dan Marino would be doing just that in the opener. Marino had been beset with foot and ankle problems for years, but he still possessed the golden arm, the lightning release and the computer brain which assessed football situations faster than any quarterback in the league. He had a good receiving corps led by O.J. McDuffie and he also had something he had not had in many years; namely, the *hope*, at least, of a running game. There was a standout rookie now by the name of Karim Abdul-Jabbar (same school, different spelling), and he was said to be the goods.

Two years earlier Marino and Bledsoe had hooked up in one of the great shootouts in the history of either franchise. That, too, was an opening game. Marino and the Dolphins prevailed, 39-35, but when that game was over people around the country knew for certain that in Drew Bledsoe the Patriots had a great offensive weapon of their own. Though a loss, the game provided much positive fallout.

This one did not. The Patriots played as if they had just been introduced on the flight down. All the cheery talk throughout the month of August was reduced to air-less rhetoric. The final score was much too kind to the New England Patriots, because the final score was a somewhat benign 24-10. To watch the game was to know that the Patriots were not really in it. The actual feel was 124-10.

"We got whipped very, very soundly," said Bill Parcells, in almost an 'I-told-ya-so' air (remember his post-Washington take), "and I know it wasn't our best. I told the players if it was, we're in trouble. I know we can do better. We'll just have to see what happens next week."

Bledsoe threw for more yardage than Marino, which only demonstrated the extent to which statistics can obfuscate elemental truths. Marino threw for a modest 176 yards (no TDs) because he didn't have to. He really did have a running game. Abdul-Jabbar rushed for 115 yards in 26 carries. He continually broke tackles. The Patriots often treated him as if he were bursting through the line carrying with him some horrible communicable disease.

How ugly was it? Well, the Dolphins had seven runs of nine or more yards and five of 12 or longer. Johnson had decided earlier in the week that they would simply line up behind left guard Keith Sims and left tackle Richmond Webb and run right over the Patriots. Come Sunday, that's exactly what they did.

"They pretty much manhandled us up front," admitted linebacker Chris Slade.

Marino had a rocking chair day. The Dolphins ran with such ease that his throwing chores were simple and limited. He had no great need to air it out, although he did complete a 52-yarder to Kevin Pritchett, just to remind the Patriots who he was. But why throw, when you can accomplish so much by running?

"That was a constant problem throughout the game," said Parcells. "It wasn't just one play; it was a myriad of plays. And it was in almost every hole across the front. As a result, when Marino wanted to pass, he didn't really have to try to make any plays. He just had to nickel and dime in the passing game which is what he did. I mean, he didn't really throw the ball down the field, hardly at all."

As for Bledsoe, yuck. It was post-injury 1995 all over again. His 222 yards meant very little. He couldn't find a way to get the job done when the Patriots got inside the Miami 20, what the professionals call the Red Zone. At a 10-0 juncture, the Patriots had to settle for a 25-yard Vinatieri field goal after running seven plays from the Miami 15 or closer, including five from inside the six. "We should have gotten seven points out of that," he admitted.

He threw a horrible interception which Louis Oliver, the interceptee, and Sean Hill, the happy recoverer of a subsequent Oliver fumble, turned into a touchdown for the game's first score. At no point did he seem very sure of himself or his offense. He threw two interceptions, but the total could easily have risen to five had Miami's defenders not been busy demonstrating the truth of the old saw which says that "if they could catch the ball, they'd be on offense."

In Bledsoe's partial defense, he had no running game. Miami limited Martin to a paltry 23 yards in 11 carries. But he had been faced with that type of situation before, and he had responded much better than he did in Pro Player Park (nee Joe Robbie Stadium) on this particular afternoon.

Turnovers are Parcells' pet peeves of pet peeves, and they killed the Patriots. Shawn Jefferson, for example, wanted to find some way to disappear rather than return to the Patriots' bench after twice making receptions and then turning into the middle of the field, where he was separated from the ball. That's twice, in the same game.

He later sustained a concussion after taking a big hit from rampaging Miami rookie linebacker Zack Thomas and wound up being held overnight at Jackson Memorial Hospital for observation and further X-rays.

Parcells summed it all up, as he usually does. "A team cannot do what we did and expect to have a chance to win. We made an awful lot of errors."

Game 2

Sport at the highest level is so often reduced to the simple expediency of taking advantage of opportunity. So many games are decided by a play here or a play there. One decision or one stroke of luck can make the difference between winning and losing.

Bill Parcells and offensive coordinator Ray Perkins thought they had the situation doped out. The Patriots were trailing, 17-10, but they had the ball on the Buffalo two-yard line with just enough time left for one offensive play. Two passes had just fallen incomplete.

What to call? Well, reasoned the Patriots' brain trust, we'll put Dave Meggett, aka Mr. Third Down, in there. We'll line up in an obvious passing formation. And then we'll hand the ball to Dave Meggett on a draw play and watch him prance into the end zone.

Good thought. Would have worked, too. If only...If only Max Lane had made the block he needed to make. If only right tackle Max Lane had at least gotten in the way of Buffalo defensive end Phil Hansen. But soft-spoken Max, the Naval academy graduate, zigged when he should have zagged, or some such thing. Hansen got by him. Hansen then wrapped up Dave Meggett to end the game and insure that the Worst Case Scenario would take hold: the New England Patriots would start off the season at 0-2.

But this game had far more to it than one missed block and one play that looked great in theory but which ended up looking very bad in practice. The Patriots should never have been in the position where one play was needed to salvage a chance for victory. This game was an unending succession of lost offensive opportunity after lost offensive opportunity, with one horrible defensive blunder mixed in.

Field position is thought to be a key barometer in any football game, and the fact is that the Patriots had excellent field position throughout and were unable to do much with it. In the first half, for example, the Patriots received the football at their own 41, the Buffalo 41 and the Buffalo 45. Potential: 21 points. Actual: 3 points. In the second half the Patriots took over on their own 40, the Buffalo 38 and the Buffalo 33. Potential: 21 points. Actual: 7.

Those are loser stats.

The aforementioned defensive mistake was a major beaut. The Patriots had Buffalo buffaloed indeed, with a fourth-quarter third-and-23 at the Bills' 37. For some inexplicable reason the defensive brain trust called for a blitz. Cagey veteran Jim Kelly smelled it out, called an audible and hit Quinn Early at the Buffalo 45. He broke free from Rickey Reynolds and galloped into the end zone for what held up as the winning touchdown.

Yes, Reynolds should have made the tackle, but a blitz on third-and-23 at someone's own 37?

"It's a little surprising we'd call that in that situation." conceded second-year cornerback Ty Law. "You'd think it would be a different call. But the bottom line is we need to execute it."

Coaching brain lock was actually the order of the day. There was an easily-thwarted draw play by Meggett with four minutes remaining in the half — a dress rehearsal for the game's final play? — on a third-and-seven. And there was a fake field goal at the Buffalo 11 which resulted in an incomplete pass when, according to The Tuna, "they made an adjustment at the last minute."

That play really bugged Parcells, who simply couldn't figure out why it didn't work. "We practiced that play all week because we thought with Buffalo's rush we would have something there against a specific rush," he explained. "When we called it, they made a good adjustment on the snap. Now, I don't know why they made the adjustment because they hadn't shown it to that point and it's not something they have a quick time to check. They had a different rush. I'm positive we didn't give it away."

Ahh, that NFL intrigue. Perhaps the simple explanation is that 71-year-old Bills coach Marv Levy just happens to be a very smart man.

The what-ifs permeated this game. Rookie Vinatieri was only one-for-four in his field-goal attempts, and that didn't help the cause, either. The kid refused to alibi for the conditions, the game having been played on a cold, wet day in notoriously inhospitable (suburban) Buffalo. Two of his attempts hit the upright.

There were some certifiably strange happenings. Meggett, normally the most reliable return man imaginable, fumbled away a kickoff at his own 15, leading to the first Buffalo touchdown. But that was a physical error, which can happen. Chris Slade contributed a mental error, the likes of which few had ever seen before.

What Slade did was bizarre. He intercepted a Kelly pass over the middle and returned it to the Buffalo 26. Thinking he had been downed, he placed the football on the Rich Stadium turf and waltzed away. Bad decision. He had lost his balance of his own accord and had never been downed by any Buffalo player. The ball was hot. Live. Free. The Bills recovered, and yet another good Patriots' scoring opportunity was lost.

Bledsoe? Don't ask. He overthrew men with chances for big gainers and he continued his Steve Sax routine on flares. He was a somber 21-for-46 for 210 yards and one touchdown.

The recipient of that 37-yard touchdown pass was none other than the long-awaited Terry Glenn. The kid from Ohio State had missed the entire training camp and the first game against Miami, but when he did arrive it was with sirens blazing. His final totals were six receptions for 76 yards, and included therein was his first career TD, a highlight beauty in which he caught the ball inside the five along the left sideline and carried a defender with him as he fought his way to the end zone with a dive.

"I knew if I could just beat him by a step Drew would get the ball to me," he said. "It was a well-thrown ball and all I had to do was catch it. I was so pumped up, I just walked off the field and later on I got the ball."

Said Bledsoe of his newest and most explosive, offensive weapon, "I know what Terry can do based on our early sessions together. He's got some speed (Bledsoe long ago earned is MA degree — Master of Understatement) and he's a very good player. I think things are going to work out just fine with Terry and me."

Grunted The Tuna, "I thought he did all right. Nobody's perfect."

The Tuna was now coach of an 0-2 team, but anyone expecting to see a reenactment of Mt. Vesuvius burying Pompeii was to be disappointed. The Tuna was actually very mellow, almost robotized, as he addressed the media immediately following the game.

"That was a hard-fought game," he said. "I thought both teams fought real hard. They're all disappointed that they didn't win, but I don't think my team could have given much more than they gave."

He sounded like some Stepford Tuna.

"I think there is something to build on here," he continued. "I think if we continue to get that kind of effort, we'll win quite a few games."

He flew back to Boston, examined the game tape and emerged from his Foxboro Stadium bunker the following morning with an equally cheery appraisal of the game, and, more importantly, what was left of a season only one-eighth in the books.

He said it was "too early" to worry about the team's impotence inside the Red Zone. He stuck up for his kid kicker, saying "he will be all right." And he admitted that, as anyone could see, enough was enough. Losing at Miami in a Jimmy Johnson *jihad* wasn't totally unexpected, and losing at Rich Stadium to the four-time AFC champion Bills wasn't a shock, but that 0-2 was as far as it could go if the team was to get its way back into the playoffs. Suddenly, the upcoming contest with the Arizona Cardinals wasn't merely a game. Now it was a crusade.

"This week's a critical week for us, without question," he declared. "I think we need to get a win, or a couple of wins, here. If we don't, we're gonna be in trouble. But I think we'll be all right. I know not a lot of people in here (i.e. the media) do, but I think we are (going to be all right). I saw some pretty good improvement. If we can smooth out a few things, we'll do better."

Parcells was about to earn his money. This self-styled tough guy, this guy who thought he'd evince a laugh or two by referring to his injured rookie wide receiver as a "she" a few weeks back, was ready to swing into his father-confessor mode. This was, he well knew, not the time to be acting like a boot camp drill sergeant. This was a time to let the team know that he had strong faith in their inherent talent, goodness and spunk. He knew he had to say this, whether he himself believed it to be true or not.

"I have to worry (about the team's psyche) at the moment," he said. "The mental thing is a concern. What you do is tell them to ignore what's going on."

In other words, he'd prefer his team not read the papers or listen to talk radio or place themselves in a position to read or hear the negative things that were swirling about. This was especially true of his quarterback, about whom the coach was becoming very proprietary. He had reacted angrily during one press session when someone asked if Bledsoe hadn't become the "weakest link on the team."

"I certainly don't think he was the weakest link on the team," Parcells snapped. "I don't know why you'd say something like that. I don't think it makes any sense."

It was a preposterous notion, of course, but the inference was not so silly. The fact is that after two weeks Drew Bledsoe looked a lot more like the battered kid of late '95 than he did like the confident, semi-swaggering Pro Bowl kid of '94. And he was still placing people like Martin and Gash in a position to make that "American League Play of The Week" on those dump-off passes. This simply could not continue.

Game 3

Two disappointing games into the 1996 season, Drew Bledsoe decided it was time for a chat with himself. First, however, he had a little talk with his father, Mac, a high school football coach. His basic advice to his talented, but confused, son was fairly simple: stop thinking and start playing.

After digesting that suggestion, he ran it by himself and discovered that both he and his dad were now back on the same page.

"I've taken a little bit of a different attitude this week," he said a few days before Game 3 against the Cardinals. "I've been thinking about how I've been throwing and I realized that when I've been the most effective, it's been when I've not been thinking. Sometimes here recently I've been trying to think too much instead of just relying on my instincts and reacting. My rookie year, I didn't know what was going on. I was just dropping back and throwing.

31

"It was the same thing through most of 1994. I was relying on my natural ability and letting my instincts make the plays. I started to get away from that last season and it's continued this season. I finally realized I wasn't the number one pick in '93 because I could go to the chalkboard and explain what was happening. It was because I had a strong arm and good natural instincts and I used them.

"I realized when I got away from that I...I...I don't want to mention any names....but when I do that I'm just another guy."

The Steve Sax thing, he admitted, was as perplexing to him as it was to everybody else.

"You could grab a guy off the street and he can throw it five yards and hit Dave Meggett and you take that for granted sometimes," he said. "I try and make it easy for them to catch because if they're five yards away and you throw it too hard it's a tough play. So you try to put a little touch on the ball. But it's something I have to be more accurate with. To say it's frustrating to me is an understatement."

It was with a cleansed mind and replenished playbook that Drew Bledsoe took the field against the Arizona Cardinals in what was, without any question, a true *must* game for the Patriots. No team starting off 0-3 was going to be a factor in any NFL race.

Remember those lyin', trashy numbers we alluded to a while back? There were more of them for everyone's perusal coming out of this game. For Drew Bledsoe's final numbers of 21-for-35 and 221 yards don't sound like all that much. Maybe you had to be there, as they say. Suffice it to say that the Drew Bledsoe personal offensive numbers did not tell the story of how much they contributed to a 31-0 pistol-whipping of the Cardinals.

Ben Coates, one of New England's most reliable receivers, hauls in a pass during the Patriots' 31-0 romp over the Cardinals. (Photo©Tom Miller)

Patriots fans celebrate the 31-0 whipping of Arizona. "I think our season began today and this is when you should start judging our team," said owner Bob Kraft after the first win of the 1996 season. (Photo©Tom Miller)

Backed by a superb game plan put together by the oft-maligned Ray Perkins, Bledsoe was in complete command. By the end of the first quarter he was 9-for-12 with 112 yards and a touchdown. He threw for three touchdown passes. He made nice play after nice play. He even picked up the team *and* the crowd with one death-defying ramble for a first down. This was the 1994 Pro Bowl quarterback, and then some.

"My confidence has been there all along," he said. "I don't doubt myself. Ever. We have been saying all along we have the talent to play and be very competitive in this league. We know that we have that talent, but when you're 0-2, you start to wonder what is going on. It was important for us to come out and demonstrate that the talent we have is not an illusion."

The Patriots hit the Cardinals with a dazzling variety of offensive plays. They threw when the situation called for a run. They ran when the situation called for a pass. Dave Meggett attempted an option pass (incomplete, but what the hell?). There was a successful flea-flicker. Bledsoe completed passes to seven different receivers. Curtis Martin scored three times.

The defense came up with its first shutout since the penultimate game of the 1993 season (38-0 over Indianapolis). The special teams were outstanding. Meggett returned five punts for 87 yards, including a 36-yarder.

Offense, defense, special teams. That covers most of it.

"This is the *real* Patriots," boomed McGinest, who had a very productive day against veteran Arizona tackle Lomas Brown. "This is what you should expect. Anything less is unacceptable. What happened in the first two weeks is gone and the objective is to make all of the teams that come here wish they never did."

It was the kind of crowd-pleasing performance that makes such a display of bravado understandable. More than anything else, this was simply a fun game. There would be more important games played in this stadium during the course of the year, but no other games in which the home team was so utterly dominant and was having so much sheer fun pounding the rival into the turf.

A perfect example was Mike Jones' Excellent Adventure, otherwise known as a fumble return with comic undertones. The Cardinals were actually threatening to score (first-and-goal at the New England five) when Chris Slade knocked the ball loose from quarterback Kent Graham, who was out there in place of the beleaguered Boomer Esiason. Mike Jones picked up the ball. And then the fun began.

Instead of just putting his head down and running straight ahead, Jones put himself in violation of one of Satchel Paige's sacred tenets, the one which reads, "Don't look back; someone might be gainin' on you."

Jones kept turning his head, and with every turn of the head he was losing yardage. He was finally hauled down at midfield after a 31-yard gain.

"They were all yelling, 'pitch it, pitch it!'" he explained. "And I was carrying it like a loaf of bread. First time I carried the ball since high school, but I should know better. When I play catch, I always catch it and tuck it, but I tried to do everything. I know my father was sitting at home saying, 'what's he doing?' He was my high school coach, and he grades me on every play."

"My advice to him," laughed Meggett, "is next time, don't look back. Problem is, ever since that Cal-Stanford thing, with all that crazy stuff, all these guys are looking to lateral."

There was one other play lingering in everyone's memory, and there was nothing funny about it. This was a Drew Bledsoe play, except that what made it special is that it was a very un-Drewlike play.

The score was 14-0 and there were 41 seconds left in the half. The Patriots had a fourth-and-1 at the Cardinals' 10. Bledsoe rolled right. All he could see was covered receivers. Bledsoe is not known for his running, which is something like saying that England is not known for its skiing. There had been many occasions in the past when he would have been smothered for a loss. This time he pulled the ball down, turned upfield, and dived over cornerback Aeneas Williams and linebacker Terry Irving for a two-yard gain and a first down. As he arose, he spiked the ball in a rare public display of emotion. He made it all worthwhile with a touchdown pass to Ben Coates a few seconds later.

"I am not a vocal guy like Willie or Bruce (Armstrong)," he shrugged. "I feel like I have to make plays. So when I do, hey, it's OK to get excited about it.

I like to play football and get excited, and when I get away from that, it's frustrating."

It was a play which certainly got the attention of his teammates. "At any time of uncertainty and certain doubt," gushed Shawn Jefferson, "a great leader steps up and takes over." That reaction might have been a bit melodramatic, but it did make the point. The Patriots were now looking at their quarterback with new respect.

"You aren't going to see me running the ball," said Bledsoe. "That's obviously not my game. But if I have a chance to make the play, I'll make the play."

In this game, Bledsoe became the youngest player ever to pass for 11,000 career yards. But the important thing was the way he just seized complete control of the game from the first snap.

The Tuna didn't have much to say, figuring that the performance had spoken quite eloquently for itself. Anyway, he's always better at critiquing than praising.

"We were pretty good in every phase of the game," he acknowledged. "If we play like this, we can be competitive with anybody. If we play the way we did the first week, we won't be competitive with anybody."

Just in case anyone forgot.

The final verbal cap on a superb Patriots' performance was submitted by the man who signs all the paychecks. "Our fans deserve this," said Bob Kraft. "I think our season began today, and this is when you should start judging our team."

Game 4

September 22 vs. Jacksonville

New England 28, Jacksonville 25 (OT)

The 1996 New England Patriots had clearly established themselves as talented and exciting, but they were also vulnerable. Proof was furnished in this game when the Patriots damn near snatched defeat from the jaws of victory before rookie place-kicker Adam Vinatieri kicked a 40-yard field goal to defeat the Jaguars in a harrowing overtime.

Though no one knew then the precise extent of Jacksonville's improvement in this, its second year as a member of the NFL, Parcells had come into this game with no illusions of superiority. "This ought to be a good test for us," said Parcells. "They have a good, scrappy team and good talent, particularly offensively. This is going to be a good test for us."

The quarterback would certainly stretch the defense; that's for sure. Mark Brunell is a left-handed quarterback with great mobility. It is not foolish to compare him to the vaunted Steve Young in both style and efficiency. The Patriots knew there were not going to be back-to-back shutouts. *That* was a sure thing.

"We've got to score a lot of points," said Bledsoe. "They're going to put some points up with their offense, which is very explosive, and we have to counter with a good offensive game of our own. It was great to get a win like we did last week, but we have to approach our situation like nothing's changed and come out with the same intensity as we did last week."

The Patriots did just that, assuming control of the game in the first 29 minutes. But after leading 22-0 in the second quarter, the Patriots fell victim to one "Hail Mary" pass by dynamic Jacksonville quarterback Mark Brunell and very nearly fell victim to another. The defense suffered a major collapse, even as the offense was going into slow motion. There was a lot of good in this game, but there was also a lot of bad, and it was with a profound sense of relief that the Patriots accepted this triumph and moved into the bye week.

The Patriots went ahead 6-0 on a five-yard touchdown pass from Bledsoe to Ben Coates. Bledsoe was 6-for-6 on this drive. The lead escalated to 9-0 by the end of the first period and moved nicely to a seemingly comfortable 22-0 on two more Vinatieri field goals and a four-yard run by Martin on a drive set up nicely by a 20-yard Meggett punt return to the Jacksonville 36.

But things began to come undone late in the half. The Jaguars struck first on a desperation pass from Brunell to Jimmy Smith. Brunell was behind midfield when he let the ball fly. As too many Patriots busied themselves trying for the interception, the ball deflected to-

New England offensive lineman William Roberts blocks an onrushing Jacksonville defender in the Patriots' 28-25 win. Roberts was a member of Bill Parcells' Super Bowl-winning New York Giants teams. (Photo©Tom Miller)

ward Willie Clay. As he fell, the ball deflected off his leg and was caught in the air by Smith for a somewhat bizarre touchdown. Rather than trodding forlornly into the locker room with no points on the board, the Jaguars instead went into the locker room with smiles plastered on their faces because they knew they were still very much in the game.

Brunell was the man most energized. Before his adventuresome afternoon's work was complete, he would throw for 432 yards and three touchdowns. He really went after the Patriots in the second half, first connecting with Andre Rison (file that name) for a 41-yard touchdown

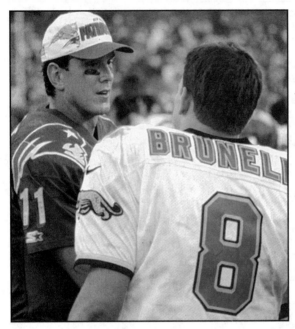

Drew Bledsoe and Jacksonville quarterback Mark Brunell meet after the Patriots' 28-25 win. Few would have predicted the teams' meeting in January for the AFC championship. (Photo©Tom Miller)

pass to make it 22-14 and then finding Rison again for a 61-yarder which made it 25-22 early in the fourth quarter. But the most dramatic play came on the final series of regulation. With eight seconds left, Brunell threw another "Hail Mary" toward the end zone. Somehow, some way, Willie Jackson emerged from the pile with the football. But the officials said he was a foot or so shy of the end zone as he lay on the Foxboro Stadium grass. No amount of Jacksonville pleading could alter that crucial decision. Instead of a Jacksonville victory, the teams were heading to overtime.

"When you're home you get that call," said Jackson, who may very well have been right. "I reached up with one hand and when I twisted and landed, the ball was in my chest and my body was over the line."

Vinatieri ended the suspense when he nailed a 40-yarder for his first NFL game-winning kick. The key play on the winning drive was a 32-yard Bledsoe-to-Glenn collaboration. For perhaps the first time in what we can safely call the Ben Coates Era, the big fella was not the primary Bledsoe target in this time of peril. Only three games into his professional career, and despite experiencing all this on-the-job training devoid of any exhibition game experience, Terry Glenn — "she" — had become a truly indispensable member of the New England Patriots.

Coates was totally nonplussed. "That's what we need to do to continue to get me open," he reasoned. "If Glenn (6 catches, 89 yards) and Shawn Jefferson (6 catches, 57 yards) keep playing like that, defenses gotta start playing cover 2 (looser zones), sooner or later. I'll get it in some crunch situations. They can't continue to double me inside all the time. When they don't, I'll be the Old Guy, just taking what I can get. I just gotta move over a little."

"I felt on film their defensive backs were more aggressive than the ones I've faced," said Glenn. "I thought they'd say, 'This is a rookie, so let's beat up on him.' When they kept Ben double-covered, it left me out there one-on-one. But as the game goes along, once you show you're capable of making big plays, they get defensive a lot."

"He is showing me more and everybody else more every week that he is a great football player," lauded Bledsoe, the man who makes the final decision on just who will get the precious pigskin. "He is a guy I have all kinds of confidence throwing the ball to. He's a playmaker. It doesn't take much to get me to throw you the ball. All you've got to do is make plays. They couldn't cover him all day."

The final hero was Vinatieri, who needed to do something big in order to reassure the mentor that he had done the right thing in selecting him over the savvy veteran Bahr. Without his right foot, the Patriots would not have won. Five field goals were enough to get everyone's attention, but the last one was the one he *really* needed in order to make himself one of the gang.

"I'm sure he was shaking mentally," joshed the great Bruce Armstrong, the sees-all-and-says-all offensive tackle. "But he might have been shaking physically if he missed that one."

"It felt good when I kicked it," said Vinatieri, "but I had to look up and make sure it was going before I breathed a sigh of relief."

Even though he had kicked four previous field goals, Vinatieri was not in perfectly good stead with his coach after missing an extra point and a 44-yard field goal earlier in the game. He really, really needed to make that kick in order to feel safe.

The coach was perhaps feeling a bit smug because he had made what turned out to be a very prescient decision in the first half. The Patriots were leading, 19-0, when the Jaguars gifted the Patriots with a 21-yard punt on which the visitors affixed one of their 17 penalties, this one an ineligible man downfield infraction. Parcells elected to accept the penalty and go for a rekick. Meggett took the punt and returned it 40 yards to set up a 29-yard Vinatieri field goal. "Hey, I have one of the best punt returners in the league," Parcells pointed out. "My players were looking at me on the sidelines and I said, 'Just watch what happens.' And you see what he did, right? How much did he get in addition to what he would have got? Make that the headline."

OK, coach, sometimes a draw play at the goal line doesn't work and sometimes a rekick following a poor punt does. It's a long season.

As for the "Hail Mary" epidemic, Parcells had no answer — as if anyone could. "We've been playing pretty much the same defense for 10 years on that thing, but that is the first time I can recall being victimized by it," he said. "I know they didn't do anything special. They just heaved it up there and you have to make the play. You see a game like that, and you know why the NFL is exciting. I am getting a little too old for those."

Relax, coach. You've got a bye week coming.

Game 5

Bill Parcells has a policy concerning his assistant coaches. They are neither seen *nor* heard by the prying press.

His chief assistant, Bill Belichick, was carrying the title of Assistant Head Coach, but that title conveyed no additional cachet. He was just as much off limits as the other 11 assistant coaches, even though he had been the coach of the Ravens a year earlier when they were more familiarly known as the Cleveland Browns. It stood to reason, therefore, that The Tuna should relax his policy in order that the media become privy to the valuable insights concerning the Ravens that only Belichick could give.

You could have assumed that, but you would have been wrong. The Tuna had his policy, and he wasn't bending.

"Can Bill Belichick speak to us on the subject of the Ravens?" Parcells was asked.

"No."

"How does Belichick feel about this?"

"You have to ask him."

"Can we?"

"No."

Only The Tuna knows how much he enjoyed that little byplay, but Belichick never did comment on the Ravens, or anything else, until the Super Bowl, when Parcells had to follow long-established league policy and allow all his assistants to open their mouths and allow words to come out. But something interesting was going on behind those closed doors, and equally closed mouths, during that bye week, because the team that went into that week was not the same team that came out of it.

Parcells paid all kinds of lip service to the Ravens prior to the game. "This is the best offensive line we've faced," he declared. "They're a very methodical team, and methodical in their drives," Parcells said. "They have some big-play guys in wide receivers Michael Jackson and Derrick Alexander, and (quarterback Vinnie) Testaverde certainly has the arm to get them the ball, but they've been methodical, basically," Parcells said.

What the public knew was that this was the team that had ended the 1994 season for the Patriots with a 20-13 victory at Cleveland Stadium in the first round of the playoffs. On that day Testaverde had seriously outplayed Bledsoe and pupil Belichick had done a better job than teacher Parcells. There was personnel movement, as there is on all teams, but enough of the principals remained to create something of a payback atmosphere for the Patriots.

This was the Patriots' day. Bledsoe was even better than he had been in the Arizona game, throwing for 310 yards and four touchdowns. He had again been presented with a tantalizing and aggressive game plan by the inscrutable Ray Perkins. Bledsoe passed on first down on 14 of his first 18 chances, and for the most part he was throwing to the right people in the right place at the right time. "He was tossing it left or right, to whoever was open," pointed out Coates, who had seven receptions good for 83 yards and a touchdown on this offensively spirited afternoon.

The great revelation was the dramatic improvement inside the Red Zone. Perkins abandoned the tight formations he had favored in the past. He spread the field and decided that Bledsoe was going to throw and throw and throw some more, even if the Patriots were on the one-inch line. Bledsoe wound up throwing two one-yard touchdown passes, as the Patriots threw on 12 of 17 downs inside the Red Zone.

"With our bye week, we worked on some Red Zone passes," reported Bledsoe. "And we were kind of excited about getting them into the game and seeing if our new toy worked."

But the game wasn't only about passing. Curtis Martin made the trip to Chesapeake Bay along with all the tight ends and wideouts, and he came in handy. Witness a spectacular 18-yard run to give Bledsoe & Co. a first down at their own 32 after the Ravens had taken a 7-3 second-quarter lead. Given the needed space, Bledsoe passed downfield, finding first Coates and then the reborn Shawn Jefferson for big gainers.

Shawn Jefferson (shown in the AFC title game) made up for a poor performance against Miami with four catches for 88 yards and two touchdowns against Baltimore. (Photo©Tom Miller)

This was Jefferson's coming out party. The free agent signee by way of San Diego caught four passes good for 88 yards and two touchdowns, while unveiling a thespian bent which netted him a pair of pass interference penalties at the expense of the frustrated Ravens.

Jefferson had been appropriately apologetic following his miserable afternoon in Miami, when his two fumbles killed a pair of needed Patriots' drives. He had even gone so far as to say the loss was all his fault, a noble, but exaggerated gesture of repentance.

Anyway, all was forgiven for good with this day's work. "The guy has really impressed me," said Bledsoe. "After the Miami game, I was worried how he was going to react. But he's reacted in the best possible way. Shawn is a great competitor. The guy is going to be a great weapon for us."

Parcells was generally pleased, especially in view of the locale. "A road win is always good," he said, "and they're a pretty good club." And 48 points? There are teams in the league who couldn't score 48 in an intrasquad touch football scrimmage. But what coach could feel all that good after watching his team become unglued defensively after constructing a 38-14 fourth-quarter lead? The Patriots got completely soft on defense, allowing Testaverde to throw for 228 yards and three touchdowns in the fourth period. The game should have been a laugher, but it wasn't safely put into the ice box until Corwin Brown recovered a Baltimore onside kick at the Baltimore 36 with 1:58 left. "I was very relieved when I got that ball," said Brown. "I was holding it like a newborn baby."

Bledsoe was again democratic in the dispersal of his passes. He again threw completions to seven different receivers. He even threw a career-first touchdown pass to third-string tight end/long snapper Mike Bartrum, whom Parcells had picked up when his good friend Green Bay general manager Ron Wolf had to make a personnel move at cutdown time.

The special teams enjoyed yet another outstanding day, the centerpiece being a punt block by the resourceful Larry Whigham, part-time defensive back who was in the midst of making himself into both a Parcells favorite and a certified folk hero with his brilliant special teams play.

One thing the world learned from this game: Bill Parcells and his coaching staff sure know what to do with a bye week, at least offensively. But The Tuna, though happy to be 3-2 after an 0-2 start, was nowhere near satisfied. He didn't know what exactly to make of his defense in general and he certainly didn't like the way his team had blown substantial leads two games in succession, turning a 22-point lead into an overtime ulcer-carrier one week and allowing a great offensive show to be jeopardized needlessly in the next game.

"I don't know if size is a problem," said Mike Jones. "They had some big guys, but we've played against big guys before. We expected to play a lot better with a lead like that, especially with as long as we worked in Baltimore."

The truly aggravating thing was that the New England defensive problems were most acute at the point in the game when things should have been easiest. The basic thought process in the NFL is that when you lead by three touchdowns your front people are in charge because they pretty much know it has to be throw, throw, throw, and therefore the front men can, as they say, "tee off" on the opposing quarterback.

But just the opposite was happening. When the Patriots were ahead by three touchdowns the pass rush was melting. How could that be?

"We're having trouble with the pass rush," acknowledged The Tuna the day following the Ravens' scare. "We're trying to scheme a little bit differently, but that's a problem. You start to blitz and doing all that stuff and then you get burned doing it. This is a little dilemma day for me. That's the best way to put it."

"We're not coming up with the plays we need when we need them," added Chris Slade. "We get teams down, then we let them keep breathing and breathing. Sometime it's going to catch up with us."

Game 6

October 13 vs. Washington

Washington 27, New England 22

It was billed as Potential Contender vs. Potential Contender, the 4-1 Redskins hoping to make a move into the NFC elite, even as the 3-2 (three straight wins) Patriots were hoping to establish themselves as someone to be respected in the AFC.

Neither team was thinking Super Bowl. The goal for each was the playoffs, although there were probably some down there in the nation's capital who were getting a bit carried away with the early-season success of the team. And you can't blame them for feeling a bit giddy after their team dispatched the Patriots by a 27-22 score at Foxboro.

They so often speak of a big win being a "team" triumph. Well, this was a true "team" loss for the New England Patriots. The offense was astonishingly inopportunistic, squandering a number of decent scoring chances. The defense, meanwhile, could not make a big stop when it was absolutely incumbent on it to do so.

After the game, Parcells was back in his post-Buffalo Stepford Tuna mode. "Give Washington credit," he intoned. "They played well, a little bit better than we did today."

This is about as harsh as The Tuna got in public: "We're having trouble being consistent. We had problems in the secondary, but it was the whole defense...the discipline was lax. It's a discipline breakdown."

The defense was not uniformly awful. Terry Allen came into the game as one of the league's hottest running backs, and the Patriots were able to contain him, limiting the talented RB to 71 yards on 26 carries. The problem was, as The Tuna said, consistency. Gus Frerotte passed for 280 yards and two touchdowns on 18 completions in 30 attempts. The defense was bad in the first period, when Washington went on two long drives, acceptable in the second period and just plain not good enough in the key stages of the second half.

"We're very, very inconsistent," lamented defensive back Willie Clay. "Some series we looked great and got off the field after three downs. Other series they go 10 or 12 plays against us, either running straight at us or passing up and down the field. It's a real problem. I mean, our offense played well enough to win, but we couldn't stop them when we had to."

The offense looked good enough on paper (382 yards total offense to Washington's 384), but once again the statistics were fibbing. Even by a conservative estimate, the 22 points should have been 38.

"We had a lot of opportunities to win the game," said Bledsoe (23-for-48, 222 yards, but no TDs) "and we

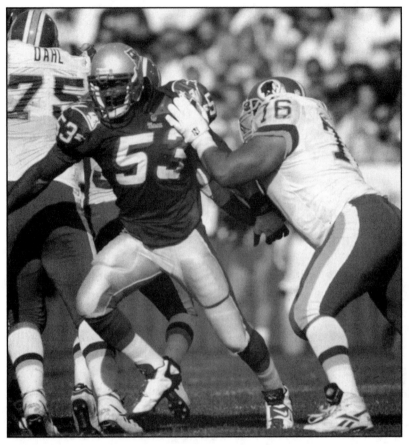

Chris Slade gets pushed around by Washington offensive linemen in the Patriots' 27-22 loss. (Photo©Tom Miller)

just didn't take advantage of it. We had the ball down there a number of times and we just were unable to come up with a touchdown and had those field goals."

Bledsoe contributed a crucial turnover at the worst possible time. The Patriots were trailing 17-16 in the third period when Darrell Green picked off a pass and the Redskins went on to score a killing touchdown. "We had so many opportunities it was ridiculous," Parcells would say a day later. "We had ample chances to score more points."

He wasn't exaggerating. "We're in the Red Zone six times," Parcells annotated. "We had at least three plays in the Red Zone what I would consider pretty well open that we didn't see properly and which forced us to settle for three field goals."

Potential in six trips to the Red Zone: 42 points. Actual tally: 22 points. That's tough to take in a five-point game.

It was a winnable game, but the Patriots seemed determined to find a way to lose this home game. There were inexcusable penalties (false starts on offense, offsides on defense, etc.) which soured the mentor's mood. There was so much bad karma that people barely noticed another glittering performance by Terry Glenn, who caught seven passes for 84 yards. Glenn downplayed his effort himself, preferring to salute veteran wideout Henry Ellard of the Redskins, who caught eight passes, good for a whopping 152 yards. "He's amazing to watch," said Glenn. "I watched him all week in film and he's still one of the best. You can learn a lot from watching a guy like that."

The loss left many of the players concerned and perhaps even confused. The team was so listless in general that questions were arising. Perhaps the team really wasn't all that good. Perhaps the defense never would come around. Perhaps all the exhibition talk of improved speed and better talent overall had been a case of fool's gold which had even managed to fool an appraiser as sharp as Bill Parcells.

"You work on things during the course of the week and it works out for you and you still lose and that's frustrating," sighed Meggett. "It's like making deposits in the bank all week and then going to the bank on Saturday and Sunday and trying to make a withdrawal and you can't. We didn't put enough points on the board. It's a team effort, but then we can't worry about what the defense is doing. We have to basically take care of ourselves. We can't worry about special teams. We have to take care of ourselves."

Speaking of offense, Parcells found himself answering questions after Curtis Martin had spent crunch time watching the game from the bench. The great running back had gained 164 yards (including one dazzling 57-yarder) before being replaced in favor of Meggett in the final 10 minutes of a game in which the Patriots were only trailing by eight points (24-16).

"We couldn't go out there and just run the ball because he was going good," reasoned The Tuna. "There were only 10 minutes left and we were down by eight. That's two scores to me."

Left unsaid was the fact that Martin is an above-average pass receiver who is always a threat to turn a three-yard gain into a 50-yard gain if given even the slightest opening.

Martin is not the boat-rocking sort, so he did not contribute much to the rhetoric. "I want the ball every time, but I believe we had to go to the passing game," he shrugged. It was pointed out to him that when he gains 100 yards the team normally wins. "First time that's ever happened to me in the NFL," he said. "You could have gained 200 yards and it wouldn't matter because when you go up against a team like we did today, you have to score a lot of points to win."

Parcells was in no mood to debate the idea, and, in classic Tuna fashion, declared the topic closed. "When you don't win the game it doesn't matter who did what," he said. "That's how I weigh it."

Game 7

When you really, really, really need a win, you take it any way you can get it.

The Patriots got this one by dodging bullets. By no stretch of anyone's imagination is it ridiculous to say the Patriots could have found themselves down by a 28-0 score in the first half. But thanks to some serious head-hunting on the part of an aroused New England defense, the worst it ever got was 6-0. And when rookie defensive lineman Devin Wyman put a hit and strip on Indy running back Cliff Groce to force a fumble late in the half, Bledsoe took full advantage of the gift. He executed a perfect play-action pass to Glenn for an eight-yard score.

Bledsoe had been informed by Perkins that the Colts' safeties were major biters on play-action, and the offensive coordinator knew whereof he spoke. "It was so easy,"

59

Bledsoe said. "It was almost too easy...I looked around to see if there was a flag or something because of how easy it was."

A 28-yard punt return by Meggett led to a Vinatieri field goal, and so the Patriots led 10-6 at intermission. Offense never had much to do with this game. When Curtis Martin ran in from the one to give his team a 17-6 third-quarter lead, the Pats then had the laughable total of 118 total yards.

The real heroes were the little-known players who helped create some key Indianapolis fumbles. There was Wyman, of course, and there was also Ferric Collons, Mike Bartrum, Chris Sullivan and Marrio Grier. These men either caused or recovered five Indianapolis fumbles.

The Colts had every reason to feel that Somebody Up There just didn't like them. They got inside the New England 20-yard line — the infamous Red Zone, in other words — four times (penetrating to the 5-, 4-, 8- and 18-yard lines) and came out with a horrifying six points. The flip side is that the Patriots were of the belief that they deserved all the credit for this startling juxtaposition.

"We were talking all week long how we were going to force things and make things happen," said linebacker Monty Brown, the team's leading expert on the subject of professional wrestling (that's his ultimate career aim). "And that's exactly what we did."

This coincided with the basic Tuna take. "That's as good a win as we've had in a while," said the man whose heart always lies with the guys on defense. "We've been giving up a lot of big plays. This time we started off shaky, but our defense answered back a little bit."

One of those defensive players admitted he had begun to take things very personally after the events of the past few weeks. "I didn't sleep good all week," said Chris Slade. "I was waiting for this game."

Injuries had forced Parcells to do some personnel juggling, and the results were more than favorable. With veteran safety Ricky Reynolds out with a bum ankle, he basically liked what he saw of rookie Lawyer Milloy, a rangy kid with some good pop out of Washington. And he liked the way the team hung tough on the many occasions Indianapolis was a knockin' at the end zone door.

"In the Red Zone in particular," he said, "I think the players were conscious of trying to knock the ball loose, and they're not even a fumbling team. When you gang tackle — and we did that much better — you normally will create turnovers. More importantly, we were able to take advantage of what we did create."

The Tuna loves it when he can get on his soapbox and say, "See? I told ya so" when one of his crusades gets illuminated. This game was a triumph of defense and defensive aggressiveness and special teams. Punter Tom Tupa, a wonderful off-season acquisition, twice kicked the ball into what used to be called the "coffin corner," and neither this nor the usual hustling efforts of his special teams went unnoticed by The Tuna.

"We played real good on special teams," saluted Parcells. "Our punter was magnificent. He punted the ball out of bounds. Our coverage was good. I feel like when we put a punt team on the field, something good is going to happen.

"I have a real positive feeling about our punt return, our kickoff return and our kickoff coverage," he continued. "And the field-goal kicker is doing a pretty good job for us. We created another turnover with special teams (when rookie Chris Sullivan forced a fumble). That's a little bit like the measles: once you get them, it spreads."

Parcells just loves to discourse on the subject of special teams, and their tremendous importance, just as he loves to harp on the incredible game-disrupting power of turnovers. "I'm just ready to talk to the team about a team (Jacksonville) that made 538 yards and lost to a team that made 200 yards," he said. "How does that happen?"

Let us guess. Could it be that dreaded T-word?

"Turnovers," smiled The Tuna, "are the most significant statistic in football, and our game was a good case in point."

So while people on the outside might think a parent would love his or her cute baby the best, the truth is that the parent often has far more feeling for the homely one. And this was a very ugly football game to just about everyone but The Tuna and his disciples. "That's what it's all about," he said. "These things happen and people, take advantage of it. I'm very pleased with the way we played in the second half. We came in here and won. Nobody else has done that (the Colts were indeed undefeated at home). I'm proud of these guys. They came in here and did a good job."

Mark that down. It was the first time in the 1996 season that The Tuna went on record as saying he was "proud" of this team.

Game 8

It might have been routine for John Elway, but it was very likely career-defining for Drew Bledsoe.

His team was trailing by an 18-15 score with 2:47 left and the end zone was 84 yards away. He was very likely going to have this one chance, and this one chance only, to get the job done and perhaps save a season.

"It was white-knuckle time; it was so tense," said tackle Max Lane, who also admitted he had no idea the Patriots were *that* far away ("The 16? That's where we started?"). "I think we knew we could do it. But due to the drives we had before, I think people would be lying if they said there wasn't a little bit of doubt. I'm just being realistic."

It was Sunday night, and the rest of the league was watching. They were watching in Miami and Pittsburgh and Denver and New York and Dallas and Green Bay and San Francisco. They were watching and they were all wondering what the New England Patriots, and their quarterback, were made of.

Among those with total faith in the quarterback was tackle Todd Rucci. "I don't think any of that (e.g. the 60,000, the TV audience, the overall ramifications) made any difference to Drew," he said. "I don't really think that was the big thing in his head, whether we were playing then in front of just two people. It was just a matter of winning the game for him."

Was it Drew Bledsoe's finest hour? Probably, at least so far. Drew Bledsoe took his team those 84 yards, with Martin finishing things off with a 10-yard run which was the key score in a tense, unpredictable and very likely unforgettable 28-25 victory over the proud Buffalo Bills.

This game meant a lot to Bill Parcells. The tangible benefits were obvious. Buffalo had come into the game with a 5-2 record and was tied with the Colts for first place in the division. But there was also a certain psychic satisfaction which touched the heart of a tried and true pro football man like The Tuna. He loved this game because he just had so much respect for septuagenarian coach Marv Levy and his Buffalo Bills.

"I laugh," he said earlier in the week. "Every year the media and the fans say, 'What's the matter with the Buffalo Bills?' But they're always there. They're always in the picture."

"You can't make mistakes against this team because they'll take advantage of them and make you pay. You have to play a sound fundamental game," added Martin.

Once again the Patriots had trouble running the ball. So it was up to Bledsoe and his receivers, not to mention his thick-necked protectors up front, to manufacture enough points. Bledsoe responded with a 32-for-45 performance good for 372 yards. Bledsoe made great use of a new target, veteran Keith Byars. The former Philadelphia and Miami star, now 33, had been picked up a week earlier as pennant race insurance, you might say. He came billed as a combination tight end/fullback, but what he really represented was a security blanket for Parcells, who adores smart veteran players who only need a playbook and are never in need of a baby-sitter or shrink. Byars did not fit into Jimmy Johnson's new system down there in south Florida. But he would prove to be precisely the right man for the New England Patriots.

In this game he got himself open often enough to catch seven passes, good for 52 yards. Much like Sam Gash, he had the knack for squeezing every conceivable inch out of every reception. "I know I have a lot to offer this team," Byars declared. "I think I might cause some matchup problems for the other teams because they don't know if I'm a fullback or a tight end. They can't load up on anything because of the way we move the ball around to a lot of different receivers."

Parcells was right — as usual. Buffalo spotted the younger Patriots a 13-0 lead, but that only served to get Jim Kelly's competitive juices flowing. He got a jump start when Jeff Burris caused a damaging Martin fumble, giving Buffalo the ball at the New England 34. Kelly then got the team not only back into the game, but right into a lead at 18-15, which is where things stood when Bledsoe took over with his team 84 yards from the Promised Land and not too much time remaining.

Suppose someone had told you on, say September 1, that there would be a key game during the regular season in which Drew Bledsoe would take his team 84 yards in 1:22 without connecting with — or even throwing in the vicinity of — Ben Coates, Terry Glenn or Shawn Jefferson? Who would have believed *that*?

But that's exactly what transpired. Bledsoe was four-for-five in this huge drive without throwing to any of his Big Three. What he did was throw to whoever happened to be open, and on two vital occasions that man was Troy Brown. He hit Brown, who had only caught one pass all season, for nine yards and for 27. He hit Meggett coming out of the backfield for 26.

But why Troy Brown? Troy Brown is a return man and special teams mainstay who occasionally moonlights as a wide receiver. He's not normally a primary target, and this was merely the most important drive of the first half of the season. So why Troy Brown? That's what everyone wanted to know. Because Bledsoe had faith in him, that's why.

"He may not have all the size or all the speed," explained Bledsoe. "But I'll throw it to him any time."

"Drew had to go through his reads," shrugged Brown, "and I guess he went through until he got to me."

"Troy Brown is the most underrated member of this team," said Dave Meggett, who has seen a few football players come and go during his time.

The ball landed on the 10 with 1:29 left and Martin lugged it home. But the suspense was only beginning, because Vinatieri missed the extra point. Then things really began to happen quickly. Bruschi harassed Kelly into an easy interception for McGinest, who returned it 46 yards for a TD into an end zone he could barely see since had been poked in the eye earlier in the game and was now playing on guts and radar. That certainly *should* have been enough.

Uh-uh. Does the phrase "Hail Mary" ring a bell? Yes, it's true. Kelly flung one toward the end zone and

More often used on special teams, Troy Brown caught two passes for nine and 27 yards in New England's winning drive. (Photo©Tom Miller)

Andre Reed came down with it to make it 28-25. One unsuccessful onside kick (recovered by, fittingly, Keith Byars), and one Bledsoe kneel-down later, the Patriots had a very important notch on the belt.

"This gives a young team like ours an inkling that things like this *can* happen," said wise old William Roberts, the offensive guard who played for both Tuna titlists in New York. "We needed to dig down and that's what we did. Players have got to realize how deep you've got to dig in this league. You can't ever think it's going to happen automatically."

Bledsoe accepted the accolades in his typical understated manner. "Laid-back" does not begin to describe his demeanor. This is, after all, the same person who would later admit to having fallen asleep in his chair while watching a playoff game in which his team had more than a little interest. "I think we're starting to develop a lot of confidence that in close games we'll come out on top," he said. "There was no panic on the sidelines. We knew we had more than enough time to do this."

For a number of reasons, it was a performance the 1995 Bledsoe could never have produced. Lane recalled Bledsoe saying in training camp that the guy they had quarterbacking them last year "really wasn't him." Said Lane, "So far this season, he's proven that."

"If you continue to affect the outcome of games by big plays," reasoned Parcells, "then you've become a dominant player."

The Tuna was happy on many levels. He had been speaking at great length about this being the key part of the schedule, because the Patriots were in the midst of playing four straight division games. Long forgotten was the 0-2 start. This was now a 5-3 team directly in the thick of the AFC East Division race. His team had come from behind. His beloved special teams had come up with yet another big game (the highlight being the Whigham downing of a Tupa punt on the Buffalo one-yard line). His young quarterback had stood tall when it was necessary. And his surgically repaired ticker had survived all the excitement — this time.

"It was like a heavyweight fight," smiled Roberts.

"As long as we are in this race," promised The Tuna, "the games are gonna be like this."

Anybody seen the defibrillator?

Game 9

November 3 vs. Miami

New England 42, Miami 23

Believe this: the Patriots never went too long during the months of September and October without thinking of the season opener in Miami.

They had stunk out the joint, and they knew it. Now they believed, we *really have a football team*. Now we've got offensive weapons. Now we've got a defense. Now we've got one of the best special teams units in the entire league. Now we've got a little momentum, with five wins in our last six games. And now we're at home.

The Tuna had one basic public comment. "If you don't stop their run you might as well not even think about Dan Marino," he said. "If they can run, they'll be able to pass."

But the Patriots were getting better on the run. Parcells had decided on some personnel changes. Gone for the time being was rookie Devin Wyman. Ensconced as down linemen were Mark Wheeler and veteran Pio Sagapolutele, a rugged Samoan picked up from the Cleveland/Baltimore franchise. The linebacking corps was coming together.

And speaking of coming together, that's exactly what the Patriots did as a whole in this game, playing evenly with Miami for a while before ripping them apart in the fourth quarter. The final was 42-23, and that was an accurate reflection of the New England dominance.

The Patriots were so outstanding in so many areas that The Tuna was even able to make general light of four turnovers. "I'm happy," he started off. Whoa! Stop the presses! "That's three division wins in a row...we did make some awfully big plays...We survived (four) turnovers...I really feel good about the win. I told 'em, we're 1-0 in the second half. My team's responding. We're still a little goofy once in a while, but they do what I ask 'em to do. We've got some guys that are growing up and Drew is the biggest case of that. He's with me mentally. He knows a bit about what I'm thinking."

This was a Drew Bledsoe showcase. He completed 30 passes for an eye-opening 419 yards and three touchdowns. It was the first time in his 3½-year career that he had gone over the big 400 mark without benefit of an overtime. And you want to talk about spreading it around? Bledsoe completed passes to nine different receivers.

Who needs a rushing game when you can throw the ball at will? That's not always the case, of course, and it's seldom true in the playoffs, but it was the gospel truth on this early November afternoon. It was another big game for Glenn, who had 10 catches good for 112 yards and one touchdown. It was also a rewarding afternoon for the irrepressible Ben Coates, among whose five re-

Miami coach Jimmy Johnson shares a laugh with Bill Parcells. It was Parcells who was doing the smiling after the game, however. (Photo©Tom Miller)

ceptions was a spectacular 84-yard catch and run for the score which made it 28-17 at the outset of the fourth quarter, when it was still a game.

Bledsoe had become a master chef for whom choice ingredients were a given. He knew he was fast becoming the envy of the entire AFC quarterback's fraternity because he had so many delectable ways to implement an offense.

"Like I've been saying for a while, we have as many weapons as probably anyone in the league right now," he declared. "When I'm able to attack, when we're able to put the ball in these guys' hands some good things can happen. When I came here all I heard was we would run the ball under Bill Parcells, but we've led the league in passing attempts the past couple of years. To Bill's credit, he's been able to mold his coaching style to the way we play the game."

There are quarterbacks in the league who would like to have one reliable receiver (Bledsoe knows the feeling himself). There are others who would salivate about the prospect of three, perhaps four. But nine?

"It's so much easier," Bledsoe pointed out. "We've got a bunch of guys able to make plays. When I'm able to get 400 yards passing, it shows we feel we have to attack. Anytime you're going against Dan Marino on the field, you know you've got to score points and you go into the game thinking that way."

This was no start-to-finish butt-kicking. The Dolphins hung around for a half (14-14). The Patriots just had far more staying power. Nothing wrong with that.

"We played as bad as we could play in the first half and we were still even," said Bruce Armstrong. "That's the way we looked at it. We said, 'Let's go out there and do it right.' The talent is here and it looks like we've matured a bit."

The word "maturity," and its derivatives, would be a steady conversational topic with this team. The fact is that the 1996 New England Patriots were quite reliant on young players. There were only six holdovers from the 1993 squad, Parcells' first. Martin was only in his second year. There were such young defensive backs as Law and Milloy. Linebacker Ted Johnson was in his second year. Bruschi, who was beginning to see more playing time, was a rookie. Glenn was likewise a first-year player, although by this time it was becoming harder and harder to think of such a productive receiver in that vein. And then there was Bledsoe, who had yet to reach his 25th birthday.

"I'm getting a sense of maturity, a sense of awareness," admitted Parcells. "Bledsoe is starting to know what I want before I ask for it. Before we get a play in, he'll be signalling in what *he* wants, and it's very often what *I* want. I think he's more relaxed, and one of the reasons is that we have a little more variety."

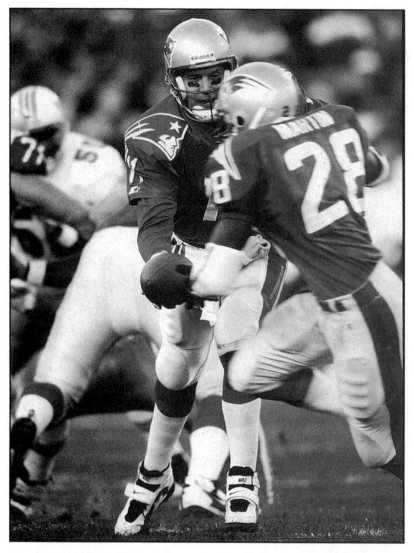

Drew Bledsoe hands off to Curtis Martin during the Patriots' 42-23 win over Miami. In one of the best games of his career, Bledsoe completed 30 passes for 419 yards and three touchdowns. (Photo©Tom Miller)

Everywhere you looked, there were smiles after this one. McGinest, now clearly on a roll that would continue right through the last Sunday in January, had another big game. Coates, who seldom reveals much of what he

Former Dolphin Keith Byars (41) was on the winning side both times New England and Miami met. (Photo©Tom Miller)

was thinking to those outside the tight confines of the team, was beaming after a big game in which he had catches of 23 and 84 yards for touchdowns. With the new emphasis on Glenn, teams were starting to forget about the man who had been Bledsoe's major target for three seasons. "They still have to stop him because he's such a great weapon," said Bledsoe, "but they also have to stop our other weapons. Anytime you throw the ball five yards and he goes off, the same thing happened on my first

NFL touchdown. It was a pass in the flat at Buffalo and he outran their players. He has great speed and that's why he's been in the Pro Bowl the past couple of years."

And Keith Byars was perhaps the happiest man of all. Let's not forget where he came from. That opening game seemed like 17 lifetimes ago. There was no longer any doubt which was the better team, and Byars was the perfect judge. "I'm the only man here who was on the winning side in *both* games," he pointed out.

Parcells was now somewhat used to the idea that his hopes and ambitions for this team might be realized. He could see the good things now, but he was far too much of an experienced coach to look at the glass as anywhere near completely full. A man who has won two Super Bowls understands the difference between acceptable and superior and between good and great. Pleased though he was, The Tuna was not about to celebrate too much.

"Just because you win a few games...what is it, five out of six or six out of seven? That doesn't faze me, because I know what reality is," he said. "What I do know is that nobody in our division, other than the Jets, can have the upper hand in division wins on us. And that's important down the road. If we can win the rest of our division games, we'll be in good shape."

Game 10

November 10 at New York Jets

New England 31, New York 27

There are but two kinds of people in this world.

The first are the people who look at a team with a 1-8 record after nine games and say, "Aren't we lucky to be playing *them*?"

The second are the people who look at a team with a 1-8 record after nine games and say, "Oh, God, I'd rather be playing *anybody* but them."

Football coaches being worry-warts and pessimists by nature, can you guess where Bill Parcells lined up on *this* one?

Parcells Sings Jets' Praises

That was the headline in the *Boston Globe* on the morning of the first Jets game. Big surprise. When the average person looked at the New York Jets he or she saw a sad-sack team with a pathetic heritage led by a friendly, but forlorn coach. Rich Kotite was Mr. Hapless. He had come to the Jets after losing his final seven games in Philadelphia. He had been hired because there was one man on earth who thought that hiring Rich Kotite would solve all his organizational problems, and that man was Jets owner Leon Hess.

When the average person looked at the Jets he or she saw a team that specialized in self-destruction. They were a team that appeared to be constitutionally incapable of doing the right thing at the right time against anybody. He or she saw a team that was a Parcells nightmare, a team which continually undid long minutes of good work with costly turnovers of every description.

But when Bill Parcells looked at the Jets he saw a team that had casually moved the ball up and down the field all season long. He saw a very good running back named Adrian Murrell. How good? "Without question, the best back we've played against this year," said The Tuna. Wow. He saw a very dangerous wide receiver in the person of number one draft pick Keyshawn Johnson. He saw some quality players on defense. He saw Nick Lowery, one of the most proficient place-kickers of all time. He saw a team that had enough talent to beat anyone on the proverbial "given Sunday," and he did not want his team to be the one on the other side of the scrimmage line when that Sunday came.

Both sides were correct. When the second period score got to be 21-0 in favor of the Jets, Parcells had every reason to worry. And when the Patriots came back in the second half to pull the game out — thanks in very large measure to the most fortuitous officiating judgment of the entire season — the glass-half-full people were vindicated. See, they said? No matter how well they play, or what they do, the Jets can't win. Period. Next question, Tuna.

It would be impossible for anyone, even Bill Parcells, to exaggerate the offensive catastrophe that was the Patriots' first quarter. Here is the sorry ledger: zero completions, two interceptions, one pass batted down and one sack/fumble. That is how Drew Bledsoe, fresh from a 419-yard performance against Miami, started this game against the New York Jets.

And then?

And then in the final three periods Drew Bledsoe rang up 24 completions, (to the by now customary seven receivers) good for 297 yards and three touchdowns.

"The key is that Drew Bledsoe had a bad start, but still found a way to win," said Jefferson. "He rallied his team to a win. That's what the John Elways and the Dan Marinos do."

The game came down to the final New York possession. The Jets got themselves to the Patriots' 11, but here the defense dug in like the Russians at Stalingrad and kept the Jets out of the end zone. Veteran Willie Clay and rookie Lawyer Milloy combined to break up a Frank Reich pass intended for Jeff Graham to preserve the 31-27 victory.

The Tuna reached deep into his coaching bag of tricks, even going to the extent of making a rousing half-time speech. For the first time he spoke to them about whether or not they really wanted to be "champions." He told them they needed to decide whether or not they wanted to win the game.

Quite aside from any other consideration, the Patriots won this game because they were luckier than the Jets. But as anyone who follows sports can tell you, bad teams always have bad luck to go along with their other deficiencies.

There was, for example, a very fortunate premature move by Max Lane on an incomplete third-down pass early in the fourth quarter. The rules state that an illegal procedure negates the play, and that's that. The Jets had no recourse. The down had to be replayed. And so on the replay Bledsoe connected with Coates on a third-and-11 at the Jets' 17 for a touchdown which tied the score at 24 apiece.

But the big break came later in the period. The Patriots were trailing, 27-24, and there was a fourth-and-two at the Patriots' 49. Parcells, who had spoken weeks earlier about curtailing his appetite for fourth-down tries, decided he had to go for this one. Bledsoe threw a pass into the flat to Coates, but it appeared for all the world — particularly the 60,000-plus at Giants Stadium, that he had been stopped short of the first down.

But line judge Charles Stewart must have been an old Babe Parilli fan, or something. There must have been some old Patriots' allegiance lurking in his heart, because he spotted the ball right up by the Jets' 49. He was admitting to nothing of the sort. All Charles Stewart said was, "I went to where the ball was and where I thought he (Coates) was." Always remember that spotting the football is the most capricious act in sport. They brought out the chains and, guess what? First down, New England.

With a skilled punter such as Tupa, a man quite capable of putting the ball out of bounds inside the 10-yard line, Parcells could quite reasonably have kicked the ball away. There were, after all, more than six minutes to go. He was even violating the very principles on which his football methodology is based, as he later confessed. "My high school coach, Tom Cahill, used to say that you never decide a game with six or seven minutes left," explained The Tuna.

But his instinct told him that going for this specific fourth down, in this situation, even with that much time left, was the thing to do. He went for it, and he lucked out.

Max Lane's false start on a third-down play gave New England second chance to get a first down. The Patriots took advantage as Drew Bledsoe hit Ben Coates for a touchdown that tied the game at 24-24. (Photo©Tom Miller)

A long time ago, some wise man, speaking of baseball matters, opined, "I'd rather be lucky than good."

"You never know what's going to happen," said Jets strong safety Victor Green. "Six minutes is a lot of time, but if we hold them right there, the game's over and our offense gets the ball back." Of course, he was speaking from the vantage point of a New York Jet. Any number of bizarre and unprecedented things could have taken place, even if Charles Stewart had grown up an Oakland Raiders' fan. But what's undeniable is that the Patriots made the most of the good fortune. Bledsoe kept moving the team right down the field, and five plays later, Byars was gathering in a two-yard touchdown pass for the winning score.

Parcells had predicted following the Buffalo game that the games would have a Perils-of-Pauline quality the rest of the way, and he must have had a game like this in mind. The Patriots came out with clogged minds on offense, the first three possessions ending in two interceptions and a fumble. But once Bledsoe got himself into the game, the Patriots began to look like the team that had just gotten through slicing up the Dolphins.

Among the big plays in this game were a flea-flicker from Bledsoe to Glenn; a clever Jefferson play in which he was able to snatch the ball away from Jets defensive back Aaron Glenn, who was 98 percent sure he had an interception in progress; and a mesmerizing excursion by Martin, who took a fourth-quarter screen pass and turned it into 31 yards worth of Gayle Sayers-like grace and beauty, during which he eluded four defenders. "Everybody was saying, 'Hey, Curtis, that was unbelievable,'" he smiled. "I'm going to have to go back and watch that one on film. I didn't think anything of it."

Once aroused, the Patriots began to make big play after big play. The offense came after the Jets in countless different ways. It had even gotten to the point where Tuna would confess that he now had developed as much personal confidence in the New England Patriots' offense as he once had in the New York Giants' defense. Now the Pats were truly getting praise from Caesar himself.

Bad first quarter? So what? The players were only thinking of the way they had outscored the Jets by a 31-6 margin in the final two periods. Keith Byars, who had started the season in the same lineup as Dan Marino, was now in the same lineup as Drew Bledsoe, and that certainly seemed to be A-OK with him.

He was still marveling about the game-winning touchdown pass long after the game was over. "It was supposed to be a corner route, but the Jets figured it out," he said. "Drew stayed with me, and I pivoted off the route and made it a square-in. Drew threw me a fastball. That had to come in 95 miles an hour. It had a lot of pepper on it. That was the only way to get it to me."

Parcells had enough 'Told-ya-so' ammo to satisfy himself. The team couldn't come back and say he was full of it. This game been dangerously close to a disaster. "We could not have afforded to make another mistake," he said. "Fortunately, we didn't."

Hall of Fame basketball player Dave Cowens, now coach of the Charlotte Hornets, used to refer to his accomplishments as "something for my portfolio of basketball experiences." This game was certainly something for the Patriots' 1996 portfolio.

"It's important that we have the guys to make the big plays when necessary, that the team has to feel something good, no matter what adversity comes up," said William Roberts.

Game 11

November 17 vs. Denver

Denver 34, New England 8

It was official now. Bill Parcells liked his team. He *really* liked his team. He was even on the verge of falling in love with his team.

For one thing, he felt it really *was* a team. He had made it clear from the start that not every unit winds up worthy of being called a team. Exhibit A was the 1995 group. "I just never felt that way about them," he confessed. But now he had seen enough. "This *is* a team," he said. "No doubt about it. We may lose what's left on the schedule, but as long as they're out there trying their best not to lose, that's all a coach can ask."

Despite their record, the Jets, he believed, were a team themselves. "I admire what (Rich) Kotite is doing," he said. "I really do. They don't have a lot to show for what they've been doing, but I have some compassion. He's done a pretty good job of holding them in there."

The more he thought about the Jets' game, the more he liked it. He didn't relish getting down 21-0, mostly via turnovers, but he did like the way the team fought back. "One more turnover, one blocked kick, one long pass, and we lose the game," he said. "No doubt about it."

But he made his halftime plea to their pride and determination and they had come back. "From the beginning, this team has done what I asked them to," he stressed. "And once you get something invested, it's harder to surrender," he continued. "The guys who have been here a while, they understand my mentality, Drew included. William Roberts, he knows what I'm thinking before I do."

Tuna reflected on the bad start. "I really didn't feel badly at 0-2," he said. "I felt we could do something. I knew these four games in our division would be important. They would be key. The division wins are very important."

He had a team that stood at 7-3, had won seven out of eight and which had a reasonable chance to determine its own divisional and conference destiny and thus put itself in place to get a spectacular trifecta: the division title, a first-round bye and a home field. These were pleasant thoughts for a man who had started off the season fairly certain he was entering his final year on the sidelines. He was starting to feel completely energized. It was as if 10 years had been sliced off his life.

He wasn't saying he had a great team, just that he had a very competitive and eminently likeable team. "We're 7-3," he said, "and, like I always say, you are what your record says you are. We still have some things to get resolved, and if we don't, we won't go very far. This isn't going to be smooth sailing. But we do have a chance to do something."

Chris Slade tries to hold off a Denver player in New England's 34-8 loss. (Photo©Tom Miller)

The Tuna even revealed a human side, as opposed to a coach side. "You get your hopes up," he explained. "I'm like anybody else. This is my life. It's what I do for a living. It's something I've loved doing for a long time. I'd like to win again. It's hard to explain, but once you've won it all, all you can think about doing is winning it again."

Now all he had to worry about was the Denver Broncos.

Somewhat forgotten at the beginning of the year, the Broncos had quietly made some personnel changes and were now arriving as the clear favorite to be representing the AFC in the 1997 Super Bowl. They were coming to Foxboro with a 9-1 record, and every football fan from Caribou to Cos Cob was looking forward to what they all assumed would be an apocalyptic confrontation of the AFC's two hottest teams.

Many were saying this was the biggest regular-season game played in New England since, well, since what? There haven't been all that many ultra-hyped regular-season games played in Foxboro, and so the answer must have been something concerning the Boston Patriots back in the '60s. This game was Capital B, Big.

As an added subplot, the Patriots were looking to do something they had not been able to do in their history. They were looking to defeat John Elway.

The Patriots were even slight favorites, and no one thought this was more ridiculous than Bill Parcells, who had never lost sight of his team's weaknesses and vulnerabilities. The public, and some members of the media, might have allowed themselves to get carried away, but that was surely not going to be the case with the cranky coach. He knew better.

Boy, did he ever.

The Broncos scored first. The Broncos scored second. The Broncos scored third. So had the Jets, only one week before. But the Broncos weren't the Jets. The final score was 34-8. Welcome to reality.

"We were completely outclassed," said Parcells. "We had no chance to win this game. This is very disappointing. I can't put my finger on why we responded the way we did. Maybe it was the pressure of a big game. Maybe we're just not ready for that. I don't know. A lot of it was poor tackling. If that's the team that shows up to play, we won't win another game. I don't know who was wearing those jerseys today. That's what I told them after the game."

Parcells himself may have set the negative tone with either a (pick one) bold, creative, curious or lunkhead decision on the first Patriots' possession, the first possession of the game, in fact. They received the opening kickoff and after three downs it was fourth-and-one at their own 32. It was a disappointment, sure, but not a crisis. Parcells brought the punt team onto the field. Life would go on. There was still 58 minutes left to play.

But Parcells had a different idea. Tupa took the snap and started looking for a receiver. He threw the ball to linebacker Tedy Bruschi, who was open at the 45. But the rookie dropped the ball. After all, his name was Bruschi, not Glenn. Five plays later Terrell Davis was taking a 15-yard touchdown pass from Elway. Forget the team. The entire stadium was deflated.

"I wanted some momentum," Parcells explained. "It was a perfectly executed play. We just didn't make the play and dropped the ball."

"I dropped it," said Bruschi, a definite standup sort. "I'm not a person who is going to make excuses. It was a big play, but it was just one play. It's one of those big moments where you have to be ready for it. I (censored) up. It would have been a big play for us."

The call actually did make sense for many reasons, not the least of which is that Tupa happens to be a skilled professional quarterback who once beat these very Patriots for 312 yards and three touchdown passes while wearing an Arizona Cardinals uniform back in 1991. Parcells had no reason to believe Tupa wouldn't deliver the mail. And Bruschi *was* open.

"There was a little letdown when we couldn't convert it," said Tupa. "It was right there for us. It was wide open. We had practiced it all week, feeling we could wait for the right time to do it. We picked the right situation. We just couldn't get it done."

But *was* it the right situation? It would have sent a message that the Broncos had better be ready for any-

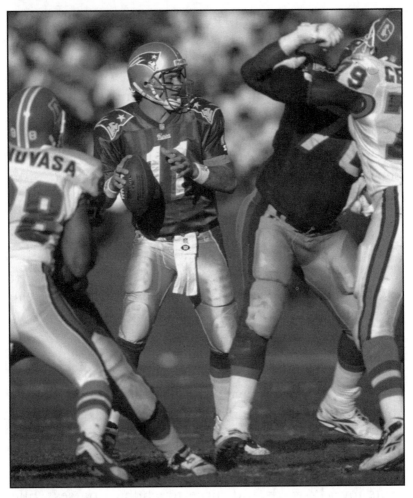

Drew Bledsoe did not have one of his better days in the game against the Denver Broncos. (Photo©Tom Miller)

thing and everything had it been successful. But in failure it may have conveyed a far different message. It may have told the Broncos that the Patriots didn't think they could line up and play with them, that the only way to beat them was with tricks and gimmicks.

"It didn't surprise us," said All-Pro safety Steve Atwater. "They run a lot of fakes. We figured they would run one somewhere in the game." Atwater downplayed any idea that the play was a sign of either disrespect or fear on the part of the Patriots. "Nah," he said. "They just wanted to get some momentum going."

As Bruschi said, that one play did not lose the game. A 7-0 deficit in the first period is not panic time. The Patriots lost the game because you couldn't pick a category in which they even came close to outplaying the Denver Broncos.

Bledsoe was back in his mid-1995 form, throwing the ball to all the wrong places. On the possession following the first Denver score, Bledsoe took a silver-handled shovel and dug a nice hole for himself and his mates with a bad pass which Atwater gleefully claimed as his very own. The ensuing Denver drive covered 42 yards in five plays, with Davis scampering in from the 10 to make it 14-0.

Just to illustrate how much this was Denver's day, Davis even scored a touchdown after fumbling. He took an Elway handoff at the two, dropped the ball, caught it on the bounce, and followed his blocking into the end zone to make it 21-0. "It was a crossover dribble," he laughed. "I was looking for someone spotting up in the corner. Then I had to drive to the basket."

The Broncos did all the laughing and all the woofing in this one. "It was supposed to be tougher than that," smirked tight end Shannon Sharpe. "They were supposed to be Goliath. We came in as nobodies and we looked at the Patriots and said, 'Let's kick some butt.' We did that. Now we're the best team in the AFC."

To the victors belong the spoils, and, apparently, the serious bragging rights.

The only sign of Patriots offensive life came in the third quarter after Milloy came up with a tipped interception. Bledsoe took the team 68 yards in six plays, with Martin going in from the seven. Byars caught a two-point conversion pass. The corpse was twitching, but not for long. The Broncos took the kickoff and went 71 yards in 10 plays, with Davis (154 yards on 32 carries) gobbling up 56 yards himself via both land and air. "We let them go right down the field after that," grunted Parcells.

"If we play like that again, we won't win another game in Foxboro," said McGinest. "We won't win another game all year. We'll be home eating our Christmas dinner again."

Denver won the total offense battle, 418-222, and the Broncos had more than twice as many first downs (26-11). The Patriots' defense, in again, out again all season, was never more out than in this game. Elway wasn't even taxed (14-for-23, 175 yards). The Broncos played the entire game in offensive cruise gear.

The game had no real redeeming value for the Patriots. The owner had to be ready to fling himself into the Route 1 traffic. "We got our butts kicked in every way possible," said Parcells. "You can put whatever adjective on it you want. All I will be doing is repeating myself. I try to put it in synopsis for you, about how I feel. I don't know what else you want me to say about it."

That's about all you need to know about the worst afternoon of football the Patriots would play in the 1996 season.

Game 12

November 24 vs. Indianapolis

New England 27, Indianapolis 13

Things did not improve quickly. Bill Parcells said the following week was "the worst week of practice for me all season. I'm glad it's over."

In that regard, he could join company with the Indianapolis Colts. They were surely happy their game with the Patriots was over, as well. They had seen more than enough of Curtis Martin.

The game plan was simple enough. Here is how it went on the Patriots' first possession: Martin, Martin, Martin, Martin, Martin, Martin, Martin, pass, Martin, Martin, Martin, field goal.

And here is how it went on the second New England possession: Martin, Martin, Martin, pass, Martin, Martin, Martin, Martin, Martin, pass, Martin, touchdown pass.

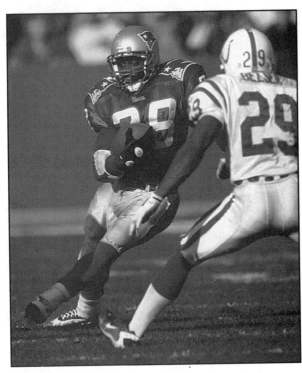

The Colts saw all they ever wanted of Curtis Martin. Martin rushed for 141 yards on 35 carries in the 27-13 victory. (Photo© Tom Miller)

Perhaps you detect a trend.

There had been much discussion throughout the season about the Patriots' difficulty in running the football. The Indianapolis Colts were banged up in the defensive line. Parcells and Ray Perkins decided to make them pay.

Curtis Martin was going to be The Man. Curtis Martin carried the ball on the Patriots' first six plays from scrimmage, not to mention 12 of the first 13, 17 of the first 19 and 19 of the first 24. "He makes defenses take notice," Jefferson said. Martin finished with 141 yards on 35 carries, and when it was all over he said, "That's all?"

The kid was as fresh at 4 p.m. as he had been at 1 p.m. This was, after all, the same player Parcells had lauded in the middle of his rookie year for having extraordinary stamina. Parcells was taken by the fact that Martin, unlike most rookies, had hit no midseason Rookie Wall. He was similarly taken by the fact that Martin was generally as good in the fourth quarter as he was in the first. No one doubted that The Tuna was fully appreciative of just how lucky the franchise had been to see this unique young man sitting there, waiting for someone to take him in the first round.

You ask yourself, "How *could* that happen?" You really would like to know how a player capable of gaining 1,487 yards as a rookie, a total which earned him the designation as AFC Rookie Offensive Player of the Year, could not go before the third round.

The answer is simple: the NFL draft, like all such sports drafts, is an inexact science. A whole lot of people messed up, and that includes the Patriots, because if they had known how good he was they would not have waited until the third round in order to draft him. The basic story is that everyone knew full well who Curtis Martin was, that he had gone to a major institution (Pittsburgh) and that he was one of the finest running backs in the country.

But?

But after ripping Texas for 251 yards in the first game of his senior year, he sustained a serious ankle injury in the very next game. That was the end of his college career. He decided not to return to school after his red-shirt senior season, and it simply appears that people were afraid he had injured himself to the extent that he would never be the same player again. Should people have done more homework? Did the player personnel directors, general managers and coaches just need more guts? No one will ever know. What we do know is that Bobby Grier and his staff thought he was a good risk. Keep in mind that a third-round selection in the NFL draft has a great deal of value. Blowing a third-round pick is not a good thing.

The Patriots took the chance, and now the team has one of the premier running backs in the NFL. He can run, he can catch the ball and he is always a threat to turn a one-yard gain into an 80-yard touchdown gallop. He is quiet, polite, deeply religious and a superb team-mate. He is a coach's dream.

On this occasion he was an Indianapolis nightmare. Things were going so well with the give-it-to-Curtis offense that Parcells was a little concerned that perhaps he and Perkins had overdone it a bit.

"He'll always do what you ask," said The Tuna, "but he's going to have a short career if we continue to give him the ball 35 times."

Everyone wondered what would happen in the wake of the Denver debacle. Would Parcells release half the team? Would he put them through four-hour practices? Would he lock them in a room and make the X-Generation kids listen to his cherished doo-wop tapes at full volume (Does anyone remember Fearless Fosdick being forced to listen to endless recordings of the "Wildroot Cream Oil" jingle?)? Would there be a Vesuvius-type eruption?

Nope. The ever-cagey coach took the reverse approach. For the most part, the coach was Mr. Silent. He wanted them to wonder and worry about what he was thinking. "The players got themselves together," Parcells reported. "I didn't really have much to do with this one."

This was an efficient, assembly line offensive game. Bledsoe allowed Martin to soften up Indianapolis before going to work. After that early running emphasis, he started flinging the ball hither and yon (to seven different receivers), finishing with 21 completions in 30 attempts for 242 yards, two touchdowns and, best of all,

Willie McGinest was part of a New England defensive effort that never let the Colts get untracked. (Photo©Tom Miller)

no interceptions. "Today was easy," he said. "All I had to do was hand the ball off, and then, when we throw, you have Sam Gash wide open."

The Patriots ran off 74 plays, 30 of them running attempts. Dave Meggett had a productive afternoon, with four punt returns for 59 yards. The Patriots had the ball for a shade over 38 minutes, their second-best hoarding job all season.

The scoring began with a Vinatieri field goal, and by halftime it was 17-3 as Bledsoe had thrown TD passes to both Glenn (five yards) and Jefferson (13). The Jefferson TD showed how far the offense had come since the beginning of the season. Bledsoe caught the Colts in a blitz, and Jefferson did what a veteran receiver should do, making himself available in the right corner of the end zone. "It was a great call by Drew," Jefferson said.

"He knew they were blitzing, and that was the perfect call. That shows you how we're clicking as an offense when we can read stuff like that and execute it as well as we did."

Alluding to the effectiveness of the running game and the overall running-passing balance, Bledsoe said, "That's kind of close to the kind of football I think Bill likes to see us play."

And did someone say "defense?" For starters, the defense held Indianapolis to less than 300 yards in total offense, and that hadn't been the case for any opponent since September. The only touchdown it gave up was a garbage time affair. "I don't know if the statistics prove it," said second-year linebacker Ted Johnson, "but we did what we had to do."

Among the defensive unit's achievements was knocking Jim Harbaugh out of the game. This just wasn't the veteran quarterback's year against the New England Patriots. They KO'd him from the first game back in the RCA Dome, and they took him out in this one with a knee injury, although the Patriots were quick to say they had no intention of disabling him.

Harbaugh was victimized by a Willie Clay safety blitz on the third play of the second half. "I planted. I had the ball leave my hand and I felt a guy (Clay) fall on my knee, on the outside of my knee," Harbaugh explained.

The defense had taken several tons of flak from the public after that Denver mess, and the players were determined to show the world they would not be responsible for keeping the Patriots from being a quality playoff team. "We were definitely licking our wounds last week," Johnson said. "We don't have a dominating defense," added Milloy. "But what we do have is people with a lot of heart."

While Parcells spared his team the benefit of his considerable powers of rhetoric during the week, he had found another way to deliver his message. He may say he had little to do with what went on in the Colts game, but the truth is that he had *everything* to do with it. Just ask defensive back/special teamer Corwin Brown, who was startled to arrive at practice on the Friday prior to the game expecting the usual simple Friday routine and instead found The Tuna there telling people to strap on all the gear because they were going outside.

"We knew this was an important week when he did that," said Brown. "Nine in the morning? That's early. We hadn't even watched film yet and we were practicing. When he did that we all thought, 'Whoa.' I got a sense then that he really, *really* wanted to win the game. We left here last week with our tail between our legs. We knew this week the playoffs were on the line and everybody stepped up."

There are no guarantees of anything in the NFL. "Seize The Moment" is the only way to go. The Patriots had just beaten a team that had come within a nearly completed "Hail Mary" of getting to the Super Bowl the year before. The Colts were picked by just about every serious prognosticator to finish first in the division. And now it was obvious that the Patriots were the team on the move and the Colts were the team on the decline.

Bledsoe had now been around long enough to understand how fragile and chancy it all is. "The difference between 8-4 and 7-5 is huge," he said. "This was a big game for a number of reasons. It was a division game. We put those guys (the Colts) behind us. And we came back after a bad game. If you lose two in a row, all of a sudden you're reeling. But we came back and I think we're all right."

Game 13

What 0 and 2?

Oh, that's right. The Patriots started out with a loss at Miami and a loss at Buffalo, and the fans were ready to burn their season tickets before the team ever played a down in Foxboro. But the coach said not to worry. The coach never panicked. The coach said that talent mattered, and that the New England Patriots had talent and would therefore be all right if they would keep plugging away.

This, apparently, is what he had in mind.

The Patriots were so good on this California night that you could say they were downright scary. They beat the, er, stuffing out of the San Diego Chargers in their own stadium. They beat the Chargers so thoroughly that the San Diego fans booed their team off the field. 45-7, 145-7, 145,000-7, makes no difference. The Patriots were pretty much playing against themselves.

The Chargers went onto that field thinking they had a pretty good football team. They weren't the team that had gone to the Super Bowl two years earlier, but they were still pretty good and they were coming off a convincing 28-14 triumph in Kansas City. They jumped out to a 28-0 lead and they had the Kansas City fans doing to the Chiefs what the Jack Murphy Stadium fans would do to the Chargers one short week later.

The ramifications were enormous, for with this win the Patriots had made it all the way back from the aforementioned 0-2 start. They were now tied with Buffalo for first place in the AFC East and they were in possession of the necessary tiebreakers. They could actually start talking about and planning on the playoffs, and not just on sneaking into the playoffs, but on entering the playoffs with the entire package — the division title, the first-round bye and the home field.

Having a home playoff game was nothing but a semiludicrous fantasy before the season started, but now it was a definite possibility and the owner was ecstatic. "I'm so excited," said Bob Kraft. "It's a wonderful thing, and this is why you get into the business. I've always said there are easier ways to make money, but it doesn't get any better than this. Now we just have to keep it going."

One man who wasn't going to be able to keep anything going was linebacker Monty Brown, who suffered a torn Achilles' tendon and was lost for the season. Aside from this sobering news, it was a near-perfect evening from a New England standpoint.

The Patriots took the field knowing the Bills had lost, but that knowledge had little to do with this sensa-

102

Defensive back Willie McGinest, who played his college ball at nearby USC, recovered a fumble for a touchdown. "There was not one guy who didn't give it everything he had," he said. (Photo©Tom Miller)

tional all-around performance. The Patriots led 14-7 after one quarter and 31-7 at the half. Bledsoe threw four touchdown passes in the game's first 32 minutes before retiring to his rocking chair. Glenn caught five of Bledsoe's completions, but this would be remembered as the night when Ben Coates reminded the folks on the Left Coast just exactly who he was. Coates caught six, good for 71 yards.

The Patriots' defense continually harassed quarterback Stan Humphries, who was also victimized by some bad drops. The gutsy QB did not make it to the finish line in this one, as he sustained an accidental blow to the head in the third quarter when knocked to the ground by defensive lineman Mike Jones. Humphries was not hit directly in the head, but was somehow conked while being completely enveloped by the Patriots' pass rusher.

San Diego self-destructed with six turnovers, and, as The Tuna always says, "Turnovers will kill you faster than anything."

There was one moment of controversy. The sequence began when Tupa unloaded a superb kick which went out of bounds at the Charger two and the Patriots holding a 14-7 lead at the time. Humphries faded back and found wide receiver Charlie Jones at about the San Diego 40. The latter made what appeared to everyone in the Chargers' camp to be a sensational diving catch. But the official on the spot ruled that Jones had caught the ball on one short bounce. Video tape evidence seemed to support the San Diego claim.

On the next play, Ferric Collons deflected a Humphries pass and Ted Johnson picked it off at the seven. Bledsoe hooked up with Sam Gash two plays later, and the Chargers were never in the game again.

Anyone wishing to know if these tales were true of a mighty offensive machine coming out of the Northeast had to come away a solid believer after watching the way Bledsoe and his mates manufactured points in the first three periods.

Perkins teased the Chargers by continually splitting Coates wide to create some laughable mismatches, and the Chargers still haven't figured out what that was all about. By the end of the first scoring drive in the third quarter, Bledsoe was 14 of 21 for 189 yards and had thrown four touchdown passes — to four different receivers. Glenn was first, with an eight-yard score on a one-handed grab behind his back. He was followed by Byars (19), Gash (7) and Jefferson. McGinest even got into the act, recovering a fumble in the end zone which made it 28-7.

"None of us could have imagined this," said the defensive end from USC. "To travel this far and win on the road and beat a good team like this handily...there wasn't one guy on the team who didn't give it everything he had. Not one."

As for The Tuna, he was already thinking about the defensive work that still needed to be done if this was going to be a viable playoff team and not just an overnight visitor. "I wouldn't make too much of this if I were you," he groused. "But if we play like we did tonight, we're gonna be effective."

Game 14

December 8 vs. New York Jets

New England 34, New York Jets 10

Now The Tuna was really delving into images.

For some time he had been talking to the team about the difference between a "club fighter" and a champion, about how a club fighter is content to remain at a certain level of competence and how a champion aspires to something greater, because, well, because he can, and, therefore, should.

After the second Indianapolis game he switched sports. He had a new analogy now, one which befits a man who actually had part ownership in two thoroughbreds. "The third month is over," he had told them. "We're starting the fourth quarter. For you horse racing guys, we're at the top of the stretch. We've got to go three wide and go to the whip now. We're in the hunt to the end of the season. No doubt about that. But we've got to win a couple more to get into the tournament."

The Tournament. That's Tuna Talk for the NFL play-offs. What he was trying to tell a partially bewildered audience was that if the team were to win three out of four games it would "get into the tournament."

Beating the Jets on this blustery day took care of the big issue. The 34-10 destruction of the Men of Kotite guaranteed that the New England Patriots, a 6-10 team a year ago and an 0-2 team after the first two weeks of the season, would be going to The Tournament. But getting in is one thing and staying around a while is another, and this is why Parcells felt the need to deliver another message to his troops.

"I've told the players you can ride down Broadway and look around or you can try to go to the show. I hope we're trying to go to the show," Parcells said.

Presumably, he was thinking about buying fifth-row center-aisle seats, and not some balcony rejects picked up at the Times Square half-price booth. He had a right to think in somewhat grandiose terms after watching his team dismantle the Jets.

Perhaps "dismantle" is too strong a word. The Patriots were not really in any serious trouble, but it did take a while to subdue a team forced to employ its third-string quarterback. With both Neil O'Donnell and Frank Reich on the sidelines, former Boston College star Glenn Foley was making his first professional start.

As pleased as Parcells, Bob Kraft and all the players were about making the playoffs, the postgame mood was something less than euphoric because this victory came with a heavy price. Valued fullback Sam Gash had sustained a knee injury and would be lost for the season. What made the affair intolerable was the fact that Gash had been victimized by the atrocious Foxboro Stadium field, and not by a New York Jet. Gash simply tried to make a move on the grass. He wanted to go one way, but his left knee wound up going in a direction nature never intended.

Sam Gash was not a very well-appreciated player by the public, because he seldom carried the football. His basic duties were to serve as a lead blocker on sweeps, as a safety valve pass receiver and, perhaps most importantly, as the man who picks up the blitzer. There was no better player answering that job description in the AFC and only one — Dallas' superb Darryl Johnson — better than him in the NFC. Parcells was fortunate to have Keith Byars around as a replacement, but he knew the team would be in trouble if Gash were forced to sit out the remainder of the season, which indeed turned out to be the case.

It had rained heavily the night before the game, and the field was in such poor condition when the game began that the true miracle is that more players weren't put out of commission by the wet grass and mud. The Jets' broadcasting crew was filled with outrage during the pregame show. When Gash went down, there was some serious "I-told-ya-soing" going on up in that broadcast booth.

The Patriots led it, 20-3, at the half. Bledsoe had thrown a two-yard scoring pass to Coates, Vinatieri had kicked two field goals and Martin would weave his way in from the 19 (his 14th TD of the season), and that appeared to settle matters because, after all, these were the Jets.

But New York battled back. Foley drove them 60 yards in seven plays, completing the drive with a four-yard touchdown pass to Keyshawn Johnson. The Jets forced the Patriots into a quick three-and-out and Foley went back to work. But on a third and 10 he found a ton of beef descending upon him and he underthrew a pass intended for Johnson. Ty Law stepped in front and picked it off, returning it 38 yards for a touchdown. "Parcells has challenged me all year to make a big play," said Law. "After I ran it back he said to me, 'It's about time.'"

The offense did what it had to do. Bledsoe was 24-for-42 for 251 yards and one touchdown. He completed passes to the usual seven, with Glenn leading all receivers with seven receptions, good for 66 yards. The Ohio State rookie came out of the game with 75 catches. The "she" days seemed a million years removed.

The outcome decided well before the game's conclusion, some of the participants had their mind on other matters. At one point late in the game, Byars, who was fast becoming a team leader, had sneaked up on The Tuna, a bucket of gatorade in hand. Back in his Giants' days, Parcells was regularly doused in these situations, usually by Harry Carson and Lawrence Taylor. But this time The Tuna sniffed it out. He locked eyes with Byars and tapped his heart, reminding the player that he had had one heart bypass already and was in no need of another, thank you very much.

"We made eye contact, and he pointed to his heart," Byars said. "He did have open heart surgery a few years back, so I told Bill, 'You've got a month to get that right. We win five more times (this including the Super Bowl) and I won't take it so easy on him again."

Once again, there were smiles all around. Among the celebrants was defensive back Otis Smith, an in-season pickup from, yes, the Jets. Apparently, he wasn't good enough to play on a 1-13 team, but he was good enough to play on a 10-4 team. "I could be in the other locker room," he said. "But instead I'm going to the playoffs."

Parcells knew the team could play better, and would surely have to play better, but this was a special day for him, and he was willing to make the proper acknowledgment. "To start the season 0-2 and then win 10 of 12 the way we've done, I think it shows a little class," he said. "I'm really proud of the players and the coaching staff. We talked a lot early in the season about whether they wanted to be club fighters or wanted to be champions. There's a big difference. They've shown me they at least want to try and fight for that title.

"Now is when it's fun to go to work," he continued. "Everyone's trying to do everything they can do to win. Everyone is hell-bent on the next one. That's why this is a great league when things are going good. The playoffs are something I enjoy. It's why you do this. Once you've won (the Super Bowl), that's all you really want to do. Anything less than that is hard for you. Still, there's gratification in seeing this team start 0-2 and then win 10 of 12."

The Tuna even kept people off-balance by tossing a bouquet at an owner the rumor mill maintained he could no longer abide. "I'm grateful to Bob Kraft for what he's put into this," said Parcells, "and he's put a lot into it."

The owner himself was positively giddy. "This is wonderful," said Kraft. "To own the team three years and make it to the playoffs twice, this is what it's all about. I was really down last year when we didn't make it.

"It's the first time in 37 years we made the playoffs with two weeks to go," he gushed. "Did you know that?"

Nice of him to point that out. But that wasn't the really big story of the day, as it turned out. Neatly tucked into a corner of the morning paper was an item that would have significant repercussions for Kraft, Parcells and the franchise itself. The headline read:

Parcells Will Stay In Coaching

It had been widely understood that when Parcells had gone into Kraft's office the previous January to negotiate himself out of the fifth and final year of the 1993

111

*Terry Glenn led all receivers against the Jets with seven catches for 66 yards,
which gave him 75 catches for the season. (Photo©Tom Miller)*

contract he had signed with James Busch Orthwein it was with the understanding that the 1996 season would be his final year of coaching in the NFL. Parcells had done little in public to have anyone think differently.

But the season was now breaking much better than anyone, including The Tuna himself, had anticipated. The Patriots were playing well enough to have Parcells thinking seriously about getting back to the Super Bowl. The things he liked about coaching were still valid. His health was as good as it had been in years. He realized that nothing he could do in life would bring him as much satisfaction as trying to take a bunch of individual football players and mold them into the best possible unit it could be.

The public conduit of this information was Robert Fraley, the agent for Bill Parcells. Fraley reported that Parcells wished to remain in coaching in "the right situation." But he did not shed any further information on just what the "right situation" would be.

Parcells was saying that he had made no firm decisions on his future, that he had made an agreement with Kraft that the two would sit down as soon as possible after the season and discuss the matter of any continued employment with the New England Patriots. He would stick to this position publicly for the next two months. No matter what issues would swirl about, and no matter how obvious it would become that Parcells was not being truthful on a daily basis when the subject of his 1997 whereabouts would come up, he would stubbornly maintain that he had not made up his mind and that the much-discussed postseason meeting with Kraft would be something of substance, and not a mere rubber-stamping of a decision he had come to long ago.

This was an issue that would never die down. It would hang over every Patriots game and every Parcells press conference. It would be Topic A for the entire Super Bowl week. It was a situation in which Parcells would forfeit a great deal of personal credibility, both with the media and the public.

Again and again he would say what he was saying now. "I'm saying the same thing (I've always said)," Parcells insisted. "When the season is over, Bob and I are going to sit down and we're going to talk. That was the deal that we made. Both of us. And we're sticking to it."

Agreed Kraft, who likewise would eventually come away from *l'Affaie Tuna* looking bad, "We're gonna sit down at the end of the year and resolve it. I'll talk with Bill then, like we agreed. Right now, my concern is the playoffs."

It was all an elaborate charade, as the world would discover in the immediate aftermath of the Super Bowl. The two men, both with large egos and both certain he knew who was Right and who was Wrong, knew very well what was going to happen when the season was over.

Meanwhile, down in the Meadowlands, Jets coach Rich Kotite was playing the Sean Penn role in a daily reenactment of "Dead Men Walking."

Game 15

Out on the field, in the locker room and in the NFL standings, life was good. The Patriots had already clinched a playoff spot. The Patriots had gone into sole possession of first place in the AFC East (Fading Buffalo had fallen in Seattle). The Patriots had a very real chance of getting a first-round bye, since they would have a tiebreaker edge with Pittsburgh, if those teams should happen to wind up with identical records.

But how good were the Patriots? Really, how good were they? They were clearly a powerful offensive team, and they definitely had very good special teams, but was the defense, you know, *reliable*? Denver was a horrible experience, and it had not been forgotten. The Broncos were still considered to be the class of the AFC. The Patriots were in a second-tier cluster with Pittsburgh, for

sure, and perhaps even Buffalo, Kansas City and Indianapolis. The Patriots had come a long, long way, but they
still needed a validation game.

Something like, oh, beating Dallas at Dallas. Would
that do it?

The Dallas Cowboys are the NFL's answer to tabloid
television. They were the defending Super Bowl champions and they were also the leader in off-season head-
lines. Suspensions and arrests and lurid tales of titillat-
ing off-the-field activities defined them as much as their
superb play. Owner Jerry Jones, reported to be Bob
Kraft's all-around owner role model — yikes! — was the
most quotable, accessible, bombastic, egotistical, quirky,
shameless, ruthless and, sadly, successful owner in the
league. Well, on this last score it was perhaps a photo
finish between Jones and San Francisco's Eddie
DeBartolo, but the fact was that the Cowboys were the
defending champs and still appeared to have the upper
hand on the 'Niners at the present time.

They had begun the season without brilliant wide
receiver Michael Irvin, who had been suspended by the
league for the entire exhibition season and the first five
regular-season games for his tawdry escapades involv-
ing hookers and drugs. Some said he should have been
suspended for 10 games. Some said he should have been
suspended for the entire season. Some said, that since
he was on probation laid down by a Dallas judge, he
should have been suspended for life. Still others sug-
gested that an appropriate punishment would be making him attend all the home games of the Dallas Maver-
icks.

They had also been hit with a large number of injuries. People, like the great running back Emmitt Smith,
were playing when they probably would have been far
better off sitting and healing. But this was pro football,

and the credo, best espoused by — who else? — Bill Parcells was, "It's football season and football players play football." They got off to a 1-3 start, but even in their depleted state they still had enough high-caliber players to get the job done. They came up with a dramatic, vital victory in Game 5 over Philadelphia on a Monday night at a time in the schedule when the Cowboys could not afford one more loss (for reasons relating to both the standings and the psyche) and the Eagles were beginning to fancy themselves, as improbable as it would seem in light of later developments, as a true Super Bowl contender.

That victory jump-started the Dallas season in much the same way the Arizona thrashing ignited the Patriots' season. And by the time the Patriots arrived in Irving, Texas, to test themselves against the defending Super Bowl champs the champs were back in first place in the NFC East and very much in contention for another Super Bowl championship.

The news was very Dallas-like. On the football side, there was howling over the just-announced Pro Bowl selections. The Cowboys had no fewer than nine choices, and that wasn't enough to satisfy anyone in the city because among the missing names were Emmitt Smith, defensive back Kevin Smith, linebacker Fred Strickland and place-kicker Chris Boniol, not to mention All-Pro defensive tackle Leon Lett, who had been suspended yet again for drug-related matters.

But the real fun that week was off the field. The name Dale Hansen doesn't mean much outside of Dallas, but anyone who followed sports, and particularly the Cowboys — in other words, everyone but recently arrived immigrants from Greenland — knew who he was because he happened to be both a TV sportscaster *and* the radio color man for Cowboys broadcasts. The latter job was the one which every male within 100 miles of Dallas coveted. Imagine. You get into every Cowboys game for free, and you get to tell people exactly what you think.

And it was by doing just that — i.e. speaking his mind — that Dale Hansen ran afoul of the owner and his coach. Hansen was a frequent and quite vocal critic of the Dallas power duo, and by the second week in December he had lost his job as a result. This was headline news in Dallas.

Another headline greeting the Patriots involved Irvin and the aftermath of his naughty behavior. It was in a weekly newspaper. The headline concerned Michelle Smith, the prostitute with whom Irvin had been found in the rented hotel room, along with the cocaine, when the Dallas policemen came a' knockin'.

Read Her Story Of Her Involvement With Dallas Cowboy Star Michael Irvin At The Hotel Room

Not your everyday fare.

There was a continual buzz emanating from the Cowboys' locker room all season, and not much of it was good. The question was just how much the off-the-field stuff was affecting the on-field play. Throw in the injuries, and the Cowboys certainly had their problems.

The area where all their woes had most manifested themselves was in the Dallas offense. The Cowboys were having great difficulty scoring points. They had been subsisting on their magnificent defense and the accurate field-goal kicking of the slender Boniol, who had kicked seven field goals to defeat Green Bay four weeks earlier.

Everywhere you went in the Greater Dallas area, the citizens were asking themselves, "What's wrong with the offense? Why can't we get into the end zone?" When four members of an offensive line that had clearly begun the season fat and out of shape were named to the Pro Bowl team, the immediate question was just exactly what was this saying about both Smith and quarterback Troy Aikman? Were these highly paid stars being singled out for direct criticism?

But so devastating was the Dallas defense that the team was normally able to squeak by with a minimum of offense. They were coming off a surprising 20-6 loss to the Giants, true, but they had nevertheless won eight of their previous 10 games despite having the 22nd-ranked offensive unit in the league. And no one was dismissing the notion that the Cowboys could grunt and groan their way to another title.

"I would not count this team out of *anything*," said Smith. "This is a very unpredictable team, but I still like our chances of winning the Super Bowl as much as anybody's."

The offensive problems were no great mystery to anyone who knew anything about football. Aikman, one of the toughest and most straightforward personalities in the game, refused to make public excuses. "Offensively speaking," he said, "we're frustrated. The way we've played throughout the season — and I don't want to make excuses as to *why* we've played that way — we've struggled."

Here are a few reasons for the offensive problems: No Jay Novacek, no reliable wide receiver to augment Michael Irvin and no healthy Emmitt Smith. There is only so much a quarterback whose entire game is built on the precise execution of meticulously constructed patterns could do. Troy Aikman was not Steve Young or Mark Brunell, players who were even more dangerous to opponents when the original play broke down. They could help themselves by running and moving around. Aikman was, in some ways, an older, wiser Bledsoe, a stay-in-the-pocket passer who would do anything he was told but who wasn't all that adept in an improvisational theater approach.

This was clearly one game in which the Patriots were not going to need a lot of points to win. The most points Dallas had scored all year in a game was 32, and that was the only time it had exceeded the 30 barrier. The Cowboys were coming into the game with New England having scored a mere four touchdowns in their previous five games. The Patriots were coming in having scored 79 points in their last two games. The game was being billed as the Irresistible Force vs. the Immoveable Object.

The shame of it all was that the Irresistible Force could easily have won this game. There was a chance to make a significant statement, and the Patriots were unable to do it. The game came down to a battle of right legs. Boniol kicked four field goals to Adam Vinatieri's two, and that was that. The Cowboys won it, 12-6.

"I'm disappointed," Parcells said. "That game was winnable."

The Patriots had early chances to score some touchdowns and thus put the Cowboys in a serious catch-up mode. Given the nature of the Dallas offense, the Cowboys might never have been able to come back. As always when a team bogs down in the Red Zone, the question is whether the offense has messed itself up with shoddy execution or the defense has simply taken the offense's game away from it.

The Patriots' frustration began on their very first possession. The defense had done its job in quasi-dramatic fashion, sacking Aikman for a seven-yard loss on a third-and-three situation, and Bledsoe had taken over nicely, taking the team from its own 35 to the Dallas four. Big plays included a spectacular, squirming 21-yard gain by Martin, a 19-yard completion to Glenn and a 10-yard draw play successfully executed by Meggett (the same play, presumably, which had failed to work at the end of the first Buffalo game).

But that's where it ended. The Patriots discovered that first-and-goal at the Dallas four was not quite the same as first-and-goal at, say, the San Diego or Jets four. Bledsoe threw three incomplete passes and Vinatieri came on to kick a 21-yard field goal.

The next blown opportunity came on the very next possession. Law had gotten the ball back with an interception, and what an interception it was. On a first-down play, Aikman hung the ball out for Irvin, a big, physical receiver. But for some reason Law seemed to want the ball more than Irvin did, and he wrestled it away from the perennial All-Pro. This time the offense got as far as the Cowboys' 13 before bogging down once again. Vinatieri trotted on the field to kick a 30-yarder and it was 6-0 when it could very well have been 14-0.

And that wasn't the last first-half chance to get into the end zone, either. Amazingly, Bledsoe and the boys launched another beautiful drive, advancing from their own 23 to the Dallas 16. The key plays on this drive were passes to Byars, good for 19 and 16 yards, respectively.

An eight-yard run by Martin gave the Patriots a third-and-one at the 16 when the Cowboys decided to take charge of their own destiny. Bledsoe handed off to Martin, but he was hit by an onrushing Darryl Woodson, knocking the ball loose. Linebacker Chad Hennings recovered, and thus either a) the Patriots had squandered a third excellent first-half scoring opportunity or b) the Cowboys had demonstrated to the world just how a defense can carry a team. In this case it was probably a little bit of both.

That was pretty much it in terms of serious New England scoring opportunities until the fourth quarter. The Cowboys weren't having much luck on offense, either, but they had managed to penetrate deep enough into Patriots territory to enable the reliable Boniol to kick field goals of 23, 36, 35 and, finally, 29 yards. Give credit to the Patriots' defense. It wasn't all a case of Dallas being completely impotent offensively. The Patriots' defense was actually playing one of its better games of the season. Linebacker Ted Johnson was making a name for himself (he would finish with 11 tackles) and Law was doing quite well in his man-to-man confrontation with the fearsome Irvin, who would finish with six catches, good for 76 yards, but no touchdowns.

The Last Gasp came with six minutes left. Trailing by that 12-6 score, the Patriots embarked on a drive which started on their own 10 and which carried them to the Dallas 23, where it eventually materialized into a fourth-and-two situation.

Was there ever any doubt that Parcells was going for it? A field goal would still leave the team three points short, with no guarantee his club would get the ball back in good field position. The call was for a pass to Ben Coates, who had come through so many times before in similar situations. But he was hit just as the ball reached him, and he was unable to hang on. It had not been a good day for him, anyway. This turned out to be the end of a 63-game streak in which he had caught at least one pass.

Parcells never second-guessed himself about foregoing the three points. "I didn't think, the way the game was going, that we were going to get the ball back down there," he maintained.

Somewhat hidden among the hard hits and near-miss plays afflicting both sides was a truly amazing and startling act by a very unlikely perpetrator.

After the second Vinatieri field goal, the rookie had kicked off to Herschel Walker. The veteran burst through the usually reliable Patriots' coverage and suddenly it was open spaces, extra bases. He appeared headed for the end zone when out of the corner of your screen there appeared a little guy in a Patriots' uniform. He was gaining on Walker with every step, and as he neared the Patriots' 20-yard line he reached out and yanked him down, saving, as it turned out, a touchdown, because the Cowboys would eventually settle for a field goal.

So who was this masked man? Who had saved his team four precious points? Larry Whigham? Corwin Brown? Marrio Greer? Which fleet renegade defensive back had enough speed to run down Herschel Walker, who, though not as young as he used to be (34), was still fleet enough to be employed by the defending Super Bowl champions as their primary kick returner?

Turns out it wasn't any of Bill Parcells' defensive backs or wide receivers, or even one of his young linebackers. It was Adam Vinatieri.

The *kicker*?

"I didn't know I could run that fast," admitted Vinatieri. "Herschel is older now, but he can still run. I guess the adrenaline was flowing at the time."

The average place-kicker is usually little more than a semiperson on a football team. He is a necessary component of any squad, but it is difficult for his teammates to relate to because while they are out there banging around, sacrificing their bodies and working up enough sweat to replenish a drained-out Lake Erie, the kicker is off somewhere by himself, or with a holder (a ballboy will do), exempt from contact; exempt, in other words, from the activity which defines this rugged, almost cruel, sport. Kickers are supposed to do their jobs and keep their mouths shut.

Now Adam Vinatieri had crossed over the line. As long as he's a Patriot, he will be regarded as one of the boys. He had done something extraordinary which did not involve the simple swinging of a right leg. Any kicker can provide three points, or one point; that's the basic job description. Vinatieri had just *saved* four, and perhaps even seven, points. That's a whole other matter.

And when the kicker in question is a rookie, well, now we're talking triple brownie points with everyone concerned.

"Any time you change place-kickers," pointed out Parcells, "he has to convince you he can do the job under pressure. That Jacksonville game was a big one for him. It was a case of 'Here's your first big one: let's see what you can do.' And he did it. So now the guy has credibility. And if you can bring something more to the table, so much the better."

Whenever The Tuna initiates a conversation about place-kicking, it usually takes about as long as Kenny Lofton to go from the batter's box to first base for him to bring up the name of Matt Bahr, a player who might rank in the Tuna Top Three, right after Lawrence Taylor and Phil Simms.

"In Super Bowl twenty-five he made three tackles on kickoffs," recalled Parcells. "When that happens, he's no longer just the kicker. He becomes a true member of the team. He's just like the rest of the players. You have to earn your spurs, so to speak. That's the way a kicker does it — by doing something extra other than just going out there and being a wimpy kicker."

There is plenty of established precedent for a kicker making a tackle on a kickoff. But Vinatieri had done something no one had ever seen before. He had gotten himself into a foot race with a man known from sea to shining sea for his ability to pick 'em up and lay 'em down. Nobody had set up Herschel Walker by knocking him off-balance and slowing him down, thus enabling

Vinatieri to catch up to Walker in a quasi-handicap situation. Nope, this was a smug Wile E. Coyote being run down, fair and square, by a lowly *kicker*. Good thing for Herschel his team won the game, huh?

No, this was an athletic feat of the highest order, and The Tuna was both grateful and impressed, not to mention shocked out of his sweatshirt.

"Sure, I was surprised," he said. "He surprised everyone in the whole world. Didn't he surprise *you?*"

The Vinatieri play, another good showing by Glenn (eight catches for 83 yards as he closed in on the NFL record for receptions by a rookie) and the individual defensive performances by the likes of Johnson and Law were the good things the Patriots were able to take away from this game. But the team flew home with heads down because this had been an exam game and the results weren't going to be good for the team as a whole.

"This was disappointing for us," acknowledged Bledsoe (20-40, a scant 178 yards, zero TDs and three glaring interceptions). "It was an opportunity for us to prove we belonged at the top of the league. We didn't get that accomplished."

"We had a couple of chances there, but we didn't make plays when we had to," agreed Chris Slade. "We've come a long way. We're finding ways to stay in there and be competitive, but we've got to find ways to win games like this."

The Tuna postmortem was fairly sobering. He felt the offensive chances were there. He was even willing to assume some of the blame — like, wow, stop the presses! — for the team's inability to get into the end zone on those first two drives.

"I'll take the credit," he said, meaning, of course, the "blame" (psychologists are invited to explain the mind-set of someone who, even while admitting it, can't bring himself to a direct association with the word "blame". "Maybe we weren't quite patient enough with the running game. That's the hardest time to coach in the whole game: it's early, and those emotions are still going."

What no one said, but what many were thinking, was that the goings-on in the early part of the game cried out for the participation of the invaluable Sam Gash. With Gash in the lineup, Parcells and Perkins might have been more inclined to give the ball to Martin and tell him to follow Gash into the end zone. Or perhaps the call would have been a pass to Gash, who never, *ever* failed to gain at least a couple of yards after catching the football on a flare pass.

The Tuna couldn't find much fault with the defense, and he thought it was time he went public about how pleased he was with linebacker Ted Johnson, a 1995 second-round draft pick out of Colorado.

"He's a good player," said The Tuna. "A very solid player. He's not a player for every down — yet — but he's gonna be on the field most of the time. I like him a lot. I think he's one of our best three or four defensive players."

The one thing that really concerned him was the fact that the entire Dallas experience seemed to be a bit too overwhelming for a few of his players. "I think 95 percent of our guys were OK," he said. "They weren't distracted by everything that was going around. But there might have been two or three young guys...this thing might have been a little bit too much for them."

Game 16

December 21 at New York Giants

New England 23, New York Giants 22

RATHER BE LUCKY THAN GOOD DEPT: Miami 16, Buffalo 14; San Francisco 25, Pittsburgh 15; Indianapolis 24, Kansas City 19

The Patriots lost, and it really didn't matter in the big scheme of things. It would have been wonderful to have defeated Dallas, especially *at* Dallas. That would have legitimized them. It might have done a great deal for unit confidence. And, yes, it would have been nice to become the first Patriots team to win 12 games. But the important goals were still within reach. All the Patriots had to do in order to clinch the division, get a home game and get a first-round bye in the playoffs was defeat the New York Giants in the Meadowlands on the following Saturday afternoon. The Patriots had their own destiny completely in their control.

But first there was the latest coaching rumor to contend with. The network TV yakkers were at it again. Parcells would definitely leave at the conclusion of the season. Kraft knew it, and had already been conducting preliminary contract talks with prospective replacements. As a matter of fact, the Patriots' job was said to be so hot that people were already calling Kraft. There was even a rumor that while he was in the Lone Star state for the Cowboys' game Bobby Grier had been talking with University of Texas mentor John Mackovic. At least, that's what the TV yakkers were reporting.

Kraft said don't believe any of it.

"They haven't contacted me," is all Kraft would say. Parcells, naturally, would say the same thing he always said. He hadn't made up is mind about anything. He said he would sit down with Bob Kraft after the season was over to discuss the whole thing, and that's what he would do.

Meanwhile, Rich Kotite was still playing the condemned man role in New Jersey and the organization had yet to interview anyone for the job.

Kraft looked weary. He was tired of talking about the coach issue and he was tired of working on the ever-present stadium issue and he said he was going to do what he's done for 26 years running. He was taking his family to Puerto Rico for 10 days. That meant missing the season's finale in the Meadowlands, but, for Bob Kraft, family had always come first.

Bill Parcells knew the drill. He knew that people would want to know how he felt about taking his playoff-bound Patriots back to the stadium where he had experienced so many enjoyable afternoons and evenings, and where, frankly, his entire reputation had been forged. And he was ready. What he basically said was, "Don't ask me. Next question."

"I really don't have any emotional reaction to it," he insisted. "That was all a long time ago (he left the Giants following the 1990 season). Six years is a long time in football. I can't say I don't have *any* feelings about it. That was an important time in my life. But I'm just concerned about getting my team ready to play on Saturday. I mean that."

The important thing, he said, was not Bill Parcells' homecoming, and it really *was* a homecoming, since he had grown up not far from the site of Giants Stadium. The important thing was the tremendous meaning of this game for the 1996 New England Patriots. The team was in the playoffs, and that had surely been the pre-season goal. But now there was more at stake, and Tuna was not about to apologize for feeling greedy.

"All the things we've worked for are right on the line," he pointed out. "We have a chance to win the division, we have a chance for a bye and we have a chance to get the home field for a while. Those things override everything else. About the other stuff (i.e. Tuna Returns To The Scene Of The Crime), write what you want. It's not going to affect either me or my team."

One thing Tuna could not help dreaming about was the idea of getting that first-round bye. Look at the record, he said. Teams don't ordinarily get into the Super Bowl by playing three games (one team which did was the 1985 Patriots, who not only got to the Super Bowl by winning three games, but who also got there by winning three *road* games). "Your chances improve by 33 percent when you have that bye," Parcells reasoned.

Again the topic of his return to New York/New Jersey for this game was placed on the table, and again he swept it aside. He wouldn't be doing any socializing, he said, because he *never* does any socializing. A road game is a business trip and it is a semimonastic experience.

129

He said he had violated that policy just once all year, that being the preseason trip to Green Bay back in August. He had gone out to dinner with Green Bay general manager Ron Wolf, who is both a longtime friend and a neighbor of his in Jupiter, Florida. He made it clear that was a very, very special exception to a very, very serious personal rule. There weren't going to be any exceptions in New Jersey. "I've told everybody already," he said. "I've got nobody to meet. I've got nobody to talk to. I don't want to see anybody."

Not even Leon Hess.

Leon Hess owns the New York Jets.

The New York Giants were a strange team. They were good enough to have beaten Dallas. They were good enough to have beaten Minnesota. They were good enough to have beaten Miami — in Miami. They were good enough to have spanked Detroit (35-7) — in the Silverdome, no less. They were also bad enough to have lost to New Orleans (17-3) a week before the Patriots arrived in town.

Though nothing was official, the coach was a lame duck. Dan Reeves no longer liked the Giants, and the Giants no longer liked him. So while it can often be argued that a team with a 6-9 record entering the final game is dangerous because the players will be fighting to impress the coach and perhaps save a job, that was not the case here because no one knew who would be coaching the team in 1997. Incentive might be a real problem for a team like New York.

And the Giants were hurt. Neither Rodney Hampton nor Tyrone Wheatley, the primary New York running backs, were going to play. The Giants didn't have that much of a running game, anyway, and they figured to have even less of one than usual. Passing wasn't likely to be a viable avenue, either, if the New Orleans game

130

was any gauge. The Giants' offensive line had been unable to protect quarterback Dave Brown, and if there is no pass protection a man can have Jerry Rice, Michael Irvin and Shannon Sharpe on his side and it won't make any difference.

Given the stakes for the Patriots, and the number of negative indicators hovering on the Giants' chart, the game looked to be a win and a cover for the Patriots, no sweat.

So what were they doing, trailing 22-0 at the half?

Here's how bad things were going: Bruce Armstrong emerged from the dressing room, gazed up at the Giants Stadium scoreboard and did a double take. He then went over to Bill Parcells and pointed up.

The scoreboard said it was 23-0, not 22-0.

"Well, yeah, simple mathematics," agreed Parcells. "A safety, two field goals, two touchdowns and two extra points. That's 22."

Which was 22 more than the Patriots had, and also 22 more than they figured to get if they didn't snap out of their collective coma. In the purest terms, the Giants had come to play and the Patriots hadn't. Hence the score.

The Patriots gained all of 21 yards in eight plays from scrimmage during their first two possessions. On the third possession Bledsoe was called for intentional grounding in the end zone, which happens to be a safety. Oh, he complained, but that was pretty lame, to be honest. The nearest conceivable receiver was in the Holland Tunnel.

OK, 2-0 isn't too bad, and perhaps neither is 9-0, but how about 22-0? That's getting a little scary.

You want to talk *deja vu* go right ahead, but it would not be wise for anyone to get cocky. The Patriots had to know that just because they had come back from a 21-0 deficit against the Jets in this very same stadium was no guarantee they could come back from a 22-0 deficit against the Giants. The Giants may not have been the 49ers, Cowboys or Packers, but they certainly were a cut above the hapless Jets.

The Patriots' defense came out with a purpose in the third quarter, but it wasn't until the second offensive possession that the offense would start to look professional. With a 31-yard Bledsoe/Glenn collaboration as the key play, the Patriots moved downfield far enough to allow Vinatieri to kick a 40-yard field goal just under five minutes into the third period. Things got a little more interesting on the next possession, when Bledsoe took them 88 yards in 10 plays, culminating in a 26-yard touchdown pass to Glenn. One of the big plays in this drive was a 38-yard reception by Troy Brown (remember Buffalo II?), who was simply magnificent with seven catches good for 75 yards.

By now the defense was locked in, and it was apparent that the Giants, absent some freak happening (a defensive back falling down in the open field, etc.) would not be scoring any more in *this* game. The only question now was whether or not the Giants' own defense could contend with the suddenly-aroused Patriots' offense.

Of course, there was one other possibility. It was now the 31st game for Dave Meggett in a Patriots uniform. He had come to the team amid great fanfare and with a bulging wallet. He was going to be both a return man *extraordinaire* and a big threat on third-down situations, either as a runner or a pass receiver. In this capacity he had been a major disappointment. He had made no major impact as a position player — none.

He was a good return man, however. Good, not great. He had contributed to the cause in several games,

Dave Meggett's 60-yard punt return for a touchdown energized the Patriots in their 23-22 comeback win over the Giants. (Photo©Tom Miller)

particularly with punt returns, but in those 31 games he had never come up with that one really big play. He had never taken it, as Chris Berman would say, All. The. Way.

But he was about to earn his MT degree. That's Master of Timing.

Giant kicker Mike Horan did just about the worst thing he could have done. He booted the ball right down the middle of the field, with little arc. Meggett caught the ball at his own 40, ran right up the middle and never stopped running until he reached the end zone. The only man who ever really had a decent shot at him was Mike Horan.

On the Patriots' sideline helmets went skyward. Very large people were jumping up and down and hugging each other. The Patriots were absolutely, positively, back in this game. They could taste that bye and they could see that home-field advantage in the first round of the playoffs.

"We had him corralled the whole game," sighed Gary Downs of the Giants. "He didn't get one the whole year long. We prepared for him, but you never know what's going to happen out there. The field was hard and slick and people were sliding trying to get him. That's just football."

"I just felt this was my house," said Meggett, who had spent the first six years of his career playing for the Giants before signing a free agent contract with the Patriots prior to the 1995 season. "There really wasn't that much emotion for me coming here. I have a new home. It's in New England. But there was emotion for the team. We were down. We needed some big plays. We needed a spark quick."

"That put gas in our engine," said center Dave Wohlabaugh.

But the Patriots were still five points down. The big push toward the much-coveted daily double of the bye and the home-field game began when the Patriots took the ball over at their own 25 with 7:08 left.

This was the Bledsoe of the second Buffalo game at work. He was a regular Unitas or Marino as he marched the team down the field, abetted by some sensational work by the receiving corps which was fast becoming the envy of the AFC.

Keith Byars eludes a New York tackler. (Photo©Tom Miller)

Glenn made catches of 17 and 13 yards on the drive. He had been knocked out of the game earlier with a painful hip pointer, but he just knew he had to heed the famed Parcells dictum about football players playing football. "It really hurt," he said, "but you have to play with pain at that point in the game."

Glenn would finish with eight catches for 124 yards and a touchdown, and in so doing he would break Earl Cooper's NFL rookie reception record. But no one really cared about the numbers. What his teammates appreciated was that he was tough enough to get the job done under personally adverse circumstances.

The drive was every bit as dramatic as the 84-yarder which won the Buffalo game, and there was a play by Troy Brown which overshadowed *anything* that had gone on against the Bills. For on a third-and-13 situation when it appeared the Patriots might be bogging down, he made the catch of this, or perhaps any other, year. All he did was make a miraculous catch practically on his back to keep the drive alive. Big? Enormous? Incredible? Acrobatic? You choose. It was a catch worthy of an ESPY, at the very least.

"I knew it was a big play at the time," Brown said. "We needed a first down, really badly then. I've caught a couple on my back like that before, but this was the biggest one I've ever caught."

But it wasn't enough to insure the victory. The game came down to a fourth-and-seven play at the Giants' 13. The Patriots had called for time just before the play. Ben Coates was inserted into a formation in which he normally plays no part. Bledsoe threw him the ball. Coates caught it around the two. There was really no way he wasn't going to lug those two Giants defenders into the end zone with him, but Meggett made sure, sneaking in from behind and shoving Coates and the two Giants into paydirt.

What Meggett did was illegal, according to the rules of football. But it's only an illegal play if you get caught.

"You saw that, huh?" smiled Meggett. "It was a team type thing. The play wasn't over. I just gave him a little nudge."

Coaches get paid to make tough decisions, and Parcells had made a big one by fiddling with his chosen play. Coates had never before lined up where he did in that formation. "We didn't improvise the play," shrugged The Tuna. "We improvised the people."

Mike Jones fights his way through the New York line. (Photo © Tom Miller)

It had been a rather classic Jekyll-Hyde game for Bledsoe, who had 12 completions for a scant 64 yards in the first half (including a brutal interception runback by Jason Sehorn late in the first half to make it 22-0), but who turned it completely around with 19 second-half completions good for 237 yards and two touchdowns.

Parcells, who had become a major public defender of his quarterback's virtue, resisted any implication that the team's first-half problems could all be laid at Bledsoe's doorstep. "It wasn't all Bledsoe," he said. "Not even the '27 Yankees could have won that game the way we were playing in the first half."

The whole thing was eerily reminiscent of the Jets game. The Giants, said The Tuna, were "more prepared to play." The team could not have afforded even one more mistake, etc.

But the postgame M.O. was for just about everyone to accentuate the positive, the coach included. For the preseason goal had not been reached, but exceeded. The team's 11-5 record was the second-best in the AFC, trailing only Denver's 13-3, and it meant that there would be a playoff game in Foxboro Stadium for the first time since 1978.

"I didn't think we could come back," Parcells admitted. "When we got the field goal I got a faint glimmer of hope just to get a score before the end of the third quarter. They've got champion's hearts. We may not be the best team, but this is as happy as we've been in a long time."

Each sport has its own inherit drama. Baseball has a special tension when a reliever comes in with the tying and winning runs in scoring position and two outs in the ninth. Hockey has sudden-death overtime in the playoffs. Basketball has a team down by one, holding for the last shot in the game. And football has the end-of-the game drive.

"You're not going to make plays like the ones we made very often," lauded Parcells.

It was a congenial, chatty, downright neighborly Bill Parcells who met with the media after the game. The man who seldom deviates from the business at hand was going to give himself a break. His family was with him, and he was going out to dinner with his daughters. "We've been going at this for 23 weeks without a break," he said. "My daughters and I are going out for dinner and a few beers. It's Miller Time."

Lessons from the Past

There is not necessarily all that much difference in talent between the teams that win and the teams that lose in the National Football League.

Does this mean some players aren't clearly better than other players, or *most* other players? Of course. In the past decade in the NFL, there have been wide receivers and there has been Jerry Rice. There have been pass-rushing defensive ends and there has been Reggie White. There have been cover men at the corners and there has been Deion Sanders. Some players have that certain *je ne sais quoi*. It has been that way since man started taking the world of sport at least semiseriously. Do you think all ancient Greek sprinters or Roman gladiators were the same?

But the overall talent gap is not all that enormous. There are certain subtle improvements a team can make which turn a 6-10 team into a 9-7 team, or perhaps even a 6-10 team into an 11-5 team. Superior coaches manage to identify what those little things are. Bill Parcells is as good a coach as there is, and he was able to do just that with the 1996 Patriots.

Should the 1995 Patriots, injury problems and all, have been 6-10? Bruce Armstrong is certainly a realist, and he didn't think so. "I think we had enough horses to win in this league," he maintained. "I honestly don't think we played any other team which had to play bad in order for us to win. I think there was never a case in which if we lined up and we played well that I wouldn't like our chances. We just couldn't get our team to play well, week in and week out."

Bill Parcells confessed on more than one occasion during the 1996 season that he was very disappointed with himself for the way he coached in 1995. He always says that no one knows better than himself what the capabilities of his team are, and he came away from the '95 season believing that he hadn't given his team the best possible shot to win, for whatever reason. He had made a vow to himself to do better, and there is no doubt that he vindicated himself, to himself, in 1996.

One of the important things Bill Parcells did was determine that his defensive linemen would be better off in a safety-in-numbers arrangement. Remember the lead-blowing of the Jacksonville and Baltimore games? Three touchdown leads just weren't safe for the New England Patriots at that point in time. And did you notice that major lead-blowing was never a real issue for the remainder of the season? That was no circumstantial happening.

One of the major reasons for the Patriots' enviable position entering the playoffs was the very considerable improvement in the defense. With the very clear excep-

Ty Law, a No. 1 draft pick in 1995, found himself in the second half of the 1996 season. (Photo©Tom Miller)

tion of the horrifying Denver game, the Patriots had learned to play acceptable defense. By the end of the regular season, every aspect of the defensive game was better — in some cases startlingly better — than it had been earlier in the season.

Parcells addressed this matter when the Giants' comeback victory was safely posted in the record books.

First he talked about how the defensive backfield had come around. In the early stages of the season the

141

secondary was often quite sievelike. Then it started to get banged up. Veteran cornerback Ricky Reynolds, a 1995 free agent signee from the Tampa Bay Buccaneers who had never really panned out, sustained an ankle injury which, as it turned out, basically rendered him *hors de combat* for the rest of the season. Parcells had no choice but to force-feed second-round draft pick Lawyer Milloy. He was always predisposed to like this kid for the simple reason that Milloy *looked* the way The Tuna thought a safety should look. Let somebody else sign those 5-9 or 5-10 safeties. He liked 'em big and rangy. He liked it when they were not only big and rangy, but also mean. He liked big safeties who really got off on knocking the snot out of people, as John Madden would say. (Steve Atwater of the Broncos was his kind of safety). Lawyer Milloy, at 6-feet and a solid 210 pounds, was in this mold.

Second-year cornerback Jimmy Hitchcock got off to a bad start and then eventually got hurt, which was, frankly, a blessing to the defense. Getting out of the line of fire at this particular time might also have saved Hitchcock's career.

The end result was that Parcells and Bobby Grier were forced to get some help, and that aid arrived in the form of discarded veterans Otis Smith and Jerome Henderson. They started to get some playing time. Late in the season free agent signee Willie (Big Play) Clay, who was only then starting to live up to his nickname, was moved from safety to corner, at least on occasion.

So by the time the playoffs arrived, the Patriots had a vastly different look in the defensive backfield. Whereas early in the season Reynolds was starting at right cornerback and Terry Ray was starting at strong safety, by the time the Patriots were to line up against Jacksonville in the AFC championship game Smith was starting

Chris Slade, miffed by a demotion during the season, played himself back into a starting role. A free agent, he quickly re-signed with the Patriots once Bill Parcells said he was leaving. (Photo©Tom Miller)

at right cornerback and Milloy was starting at free safety. And the team was much better off for it.

Cornerback Ty Law was starting to become a very intriguing player. The 1995 number one draft pick had often been overlooked by the public because he was a member of the same draft which had produced Curtis Martin, but he had really found himself in the second half of the 1996 season (remember the interception runback against the Jets and the "It's about time!" from Parcells?).

"He's really improved," said Parcells. "He's very competitive. He's got to keep his competition. He's still got maturity lapses (a fatal malady for a cornerback), but those lapses are becoming less frequent. "He *does* respond to competition, and you like that in a player. It's really a key thing when evaluating a player."

The linebacking corps was likewise solidified. Parcells tinkered with this unit during the season, with his most interesting controversial move being the demotion — there is no other way to put it — of touted Chris Slade, whom he changed from an every-play guy to a pass-rushing specialist, and then back again. Slade was stunned and hurt by the original move, but he took the high road, vis a vis media popoffs and the like. He played the good soldier, and he would eventually earn himself back into his mentor's official good graces, but he would not forget, either.

Slade was a free agent, and there wasn't much doubt that he was no longer interested in playing for Bill Parcells. When the season was over, and The Tuna had departed for the Meadowlands, Slade re-upped with the Patriots faster than you could say "Told ya so."

But whatever Slade's personal travails, the rest of the unit was enjoying itself. Todd Collins, who had surprised everyone in the organization by abruptly turning in his uniform the year before, was back and he was getting better by the game. And then there was Ted Johnson, whose ability was obvious and whose confidence was growing by the game.

At the conclusion of the disappointing 6-10 1995 season, Parcells had been asked about some of his personnel, and as he was ticking off this guy and that guy, he had said, "Ted Johnson might look different." He also said, "Willie McGinest might look different." Presumably, both of these players were looking as Parcells had fantasized they might look. By the season's end, the unit of Slade, Johnson and Collins was being regarded as perhaps the best young (underline that word) linebacking corps in the game. Their ages were, respectively, 26, 24 and 26, and they could certainly play.

But the defensive line was the *real* story. Stopping the run was not exactly a feature of the early-season Patriots, and the line's inability to keep doing even the good things it was doing as games wore on was a major concern. This is where Parcells got back to basics.

"From a coach's educational standpoint," said Parcells, "we learned earlier in the season that if we played just one unit we would suffer from a fatigue factor. We're just not that big (none of his employable defensive linemen weighs 300; there are no Gilbert Browns on this team — yet). There were a couple of games we won, such as Jacksonville and the Ravens, where we had trouble holding the lead. It was an overall coaching decision — and, believe me, there were no big arguments — to get more people involved. And it's really helped our overall defense."

Once he did that, people started to hear more about such people as tackle Pio Sagapolutele, tackle Mark Wheeler and defensive end Ferric Collons. Once he did that, the Patriots started to play more consistent start-to-finish defense (again, the Denver game excepted).

"I feel the defense has come along," Parcells said. "I don't think we're overpowering, but when we're active and hustling we can play very adequate defense. If the competition will allow us to go on, well, we'll see."

Understand this about Parcells: when he thinks about football, his favorite number is zero. Give him a safety, give him a field goal, hey, even give him a touchdown he can call his very own, but he figures he won't need very much of anything if his guys are holding the other team to nothing, nothing at all. Good, solid, slam-bang defense is what warms his heart and puts a smile on The Tuna's face.

That's what concerned him the most about the 1995 season. He knew Bledsoe had been hurt and that there wasn't much anyone could have done about that. He had been presented with a gift from the gods in the form of a near-1,500-yard running back in Curtis Martin. He already had Ben Coates. But he was very concerned about the defense. If *that* didn't improve, all the rest would be very wearying and boring conversation.

Asked just prior to the final game of the 1995 season what his team needs to do for the future, this is what he had to say: "Well, I don't want to prioritize it. But let me generally say, no matter what sport you coach — I don't care, any sport — until you play better defense than we are playing, you are not going to win. You *have* to play better defense. Anyone who disputes that knows nothing about sports. I don't think anyone would dispute that we would have to play better defense.

"You look at any sport, the most successful teams — baseball, football, whatever you want — we have to do *something*. I know where the offense is a lot more than I know where the defense is."

Listening to that dissertation, it becomes easier to understand why Parcells would react so violently when his desire to draft a defensive lineman in the first round of the draft was overruled by his owner on Draft Day.

Parcells has an endless amount of theories about football, and he believes he has as good a handle on the drafting process as the next guy, or next 100,000 guys. In the back of his mind, he always believed it would be possible to find a receiver somehow, some way, and that, in any event, it would be easier to find an acceptable receiver than it would be to find a good defensive line prospect.

"Now receiver is a position that you have some choices, usually," he said. "Because there are always a few (free agents) in the pros now and then, and there are always a few coming out of college. And a small-school receiver can play just as good as a big-school receiver, where, by and large, a small-school lineman is going to have a harder time going in."

True or false? Like most generalizations, it is a partial truth. The man generally acclaimed as the greatest wide receiver of all-time, Jerry Rice, came out of Mississippi Valley State, an all-black school in the middle of absolutely nowhere (Ita Bena, Miss.) playing in a small conference. But there was also a defensive lineman heading to the Pro Bowl *who had never played for any college at all*. That was Eric Swann of the Arizona Cardinals, whose college career never materialized due to any number of problems and who came into the NFL via the unheard-of route known as minor-league football. But The Tuna is used to dictating the flow of any coach-press conversation, and he does not like to be contradicted.

The one thing Tuna said about defense that really can't be disputed is that successful defensive interior linemen simply must be bigger than they were, even in the very recent past. "I want big fast guys," Parcells said. "Everybody wants them. You can't go in there with 260-pound guys. You can't. Nobody's got them. On the perimeter, yes, but on the inside, no."

And the Patriots *were* getting bigger, even if they didn't yet have the 330-pound run stoppers like Gilbert

Brown on the squad. Whereas Parcells had gone through the beginning of his Patriots tenure with 258-pound Tim Goad as the nose tackle in a 3-4 arrangement, now he was going with 6-foot, 6-inch, 295-pound Pio Sagapolutele and 6-foot, 3-inch, 285-pound Mark Wheeler as his primary defensive tackles. And rushing from the left side on most occasions was 6-foot, 6-inch, 285-pound third-year defensive end Ferric Collons. Things *were* improving, size-wise.

Another great area of concern for Parcells as he examined the 1995 season was the kicking game. He was not thrilled with the punting of either Pat O'Neill (released after Game 8) or replacement Bryan Wagner, and he knew that the end for his beloved Matt Bahr was very near. He had no real way of knowing at this juncture that Tom Tupa would come in from Cleveland and give him a first-class punting season or that a little kid from South Dakota State would displace Bahr and go on to score 120 points while making good on 27 of 35 field goals (About those three missed extra points, Shhh!)

People were making the inevitable comparisons to the 1994 team, which had gone into the playoffs with high hopes, only to be knocked out in the wild-card game by a Cleveland team coached, interestingly, by current assistant head coach Bill Belichick. Upon closer examination, however, there really wasn't all that much of a comparison. This was clearly a better team.

The 1994 team came into the playoffs on a roll; no one was disputing that. After nine games the team was 3-6 and was tumbling. They had lost four in a row, and the last thing anyone was thinking about was a playoff game.

The season turned around in highly dramatic fashion on the 13th of November. Very late in the second quarter the season seemed irretrievably lost. The Vikings had a 20-0 lead and were in complete control.

But Bledsoe completed four passes in the final minute and Matt Bahr kicked a 38-yard field goal with no time left to send the Patriots into the locker room with a faint pulse.

Bledsoe hit Ray Crittenden for a 31-yard touchdown pass to start the second half, and from then on he was not an NFL quarterback. Rather, he was a son of Zeus sent from Mt. Olympus to resuscitate the franchise. He completed 37 of 53 passes for 354 yards in the second half and overtime alone. His final totals of 70 attempts and 45 completions are NFL records. In the overtime it was clear that Drew Bledsoe wasn't going to settle for winning this by some weenie field goal. He completed his first five passes and eventually found Kevin Turner in the corner of the end zone for the game-winning touchdown.

That was the start of a seven-game winning streak. The Patriots went into the last two weeks of the season needing road victories in both Buffalo and Chicago to get into the playoffs. They destroyed the Bills 41-17 and then handled the Bears, 13-3. At this point they were feeling invincible.

They had drawn Cleveland, at Cleveland, and they weren't too worried. The Browns had beaten them, 13-6 in Week 9. That had been the final loss of the four-game losing streak. The Patriots thought they were so much better now that they were privately starting to wonder why the Browns would even bother to show up.

Before 77,452 in historic Cleveland Stadium, the Patriots found out what the playoffs were all about. Vinnie Testaverde picked them apart, while the Belichick defense took care of Bledsoe, who eliminated just about any victory chances the Patriots had with a pair of damaging second-half interceptions. The Patriots had their chances in the second half, but when it was all over the

Browns had won, 20-13, and there had really been no doubt which was the more mature and more deserving team.

Gifted with 20-20 hindsight two years later, those who were there realized some things they had been too blind to see at the time. Start with the basic fact that the team had gone into the playoffs riding that seven-game winning streak. That may sound good, but it was not a realistic evaluation of how good the team really was. Bruce Armstrong was among those who recognized that in order for the Patriots to win the Super Bowl in 1994-95 they would have needed an 11-game winning streak, the last four of which were playoff games. They would play zero home games. That was dreaming. Few teams are that good at any time, and the 1994 New England Patriots were nowhere near that good.

"We're off the first week," pointed out Armstrong. "Then we play at home. If Denver falls, we would be at home again. If not, we have a challenge, but it's something we could do."

The 1994 Patriots were utterly one-dimensional. Take away the pass, and you had the Patriots. The leading rusher that season was Marion Butts, a bruising north-south runner Parcells had imported from San Diego, where once upon a time he had been a 1,000-yard rusher. But as a Patriot, he was mediocrity. He huffed and puffed his way to 703 yards, averaging fewer than three yards a carry. And when the playoff game arrived, he was removed from the lineup in favor of Corey Croom, who had not carried the ball even once from scrimmage all year.

In other words, there was no Curtis Martin on *that* team.

In many other ways the talent upgrade was significant. McGinest was just a rookie part-time player that year. Now he was developing into one of the better pass-rushing defensive ends in the game. There were no young talents such as Law and Milloy in the defensive backfield, either. There really was no comparison between the teams. The '96 team would have wiped the floor with the '94 team.

The Tuna even admitted something that must have been very hard for him to spit out. He actually admitted to fallibility. He confessed to a disbelieving press corps that, on top of any other deficiencies the team might have had against Cleveland that day, he had not coached very well, either.

"I think we made a mistake of adding a few too many things for Drew in that game," said Parcells. "And we just didn't execute well at all. I take responsibility for that. We tried to change some of his reads, because we thought he could handle it. We were playing a real good defensive team with some great pressure players who just didn't take chances. You look back later and say to yourself, 'What did *you* do that day?' and I think I made a mistake."

The Tuna said he really didn't enter that playoff game in Cleveland infused with confidence, at least in terms of offense. "I remember going into that game in Cleveland thinking it was basically a Coates-(Kevin) Turner-(Leroy) Thompson thing," he said. "And I was maybe hoping (wide receiver) Michael Timpson would come up with a big play — something like that. But, basically, we were a tight end-fullback team."

There wasn't doubt that he was taking a far more versatile offensive machine into these playoffs. "I feel this time we are a much more explosive team," Parcells said. "You just can't let anybody loose. Bledsoe can hurt you. Martin can hurt you. Coates can hurt you. Jefferson can hurt you. Byars can hurt you. But, of course, we still have to block 'em, and that can be negated."

He stressed once again that this was a team he could live with. He liked the way it continually bounced back from negative happenings, such as the 0-2 start, the disappointment of the Redskins' game and the horror of Denver. "They don't have long memories for negative things," he said. He praised the way the players have reacted to coaching. "Whatever I've asked them to do, they've done," he said.

The Patriots were always going to have a problem playing for Parcells because he had been to the mountain top twice before with teams that had given him the most immense satisfactions a coach could have. The Tuna didn't have to guess about the possibilities inherent in his chosen sport; he *knew*. Those Giants' teams had raised the bar for him, and for all teams he would coach in the future.

So any time he admitted publicly that any individual, or any aspect of the team's overall performance, was reminiscent of something that he had known with the Giants (such as when he had declared that he had developed as much confidence in the Patriots' offense as he once had in the Giants' defense), it was big local media news indeed. Giants' comparisons were precious, and he did not dole them out indiscriminately.

As the season wore on, he started to soften. He would get to the point where he was talking about the love and respect he had for this team, and he was even comparing its trek toward the Super Bowl to one of those old New York trips. "They've paid the same price," he said. "Same sweat. Same blood. Same turned ankles. Same IVs on the plane coming home. It's all the same."

And this: "These kids have champions' hearts," he said. "And they are mentally tough."

They were going to need every bit of that mental toughness, because for a first-round opponent they had drawn the proud Pittsburgh Steelers, who, until further notice, just happened to be the defending American Football Conference champions.

The Playoffs

January 5, 1997 vs. Pittsburgh

New England 28, Pittsburgh 3

It's not easy to be a Pittsburgh Steeler. Every time you go to work you are confronted with the burden of history.

Life for any sort of defending champion is rough, as the Patriots themselves would find out in 1997. But it's far worse in Pittsburgh, where there are all kinds of devoted fans who have vivid memories of just about every snap of the ball during the four seasons in the 1970s when the Steelers won the Super Bowl. The contemporary Steelers must walk past four gleaming silver Super Bowl trophies as they walk through the lobby at Three Rivers Stadium, where they practice during the regular season.

The Steelers had gotten back to the Super Bowl in 1996. They had won the AFC in a wild-and-wooly Adventure Theatre special with Indianapolis, a game that wasn't decided until an Indianapolis "Hail Mary" — there's that phrase again — pass fell to the turf on the final play of the game. They played a good enough game in the Super Bowl to win a lot of Super Bowls. Were it not for two inexplicably horrible interceptions thrown by quarterback Neil O'Donnell, they might very well have won it.

O'Donnell had taken the money, $25 million worth, and had skipped off to join the Jets while the personal going was good and the Leon Hess ATM machine was running, but the Steelers had rallied behind journeyman quarterback Mike Tomczak to go 10-6 and win the AFC Central. They had made one truly superb move during the off-season, making a great draft day trade with the St. Louis Rams for bruising running back Jerome Bettis and the 250-pound bowling ball had responded by gaining 1,431 yards.

The Steelers have one of the great fanatical fandoms in all of sport, let alone the NFL. Though times have changed and the steel mills have closed, the image of this town as a haven for red, white and blue, 100 percent rugged, no-nonsense Americans holds true. For people of that substance and fiber, football is the perfect game, and the Steelers are the beneficiaries of a passionate following. You don't need any three, four, five or six degrees of separation in any Pittsburgh-area family in order to find someone who dreams of seeing the glories of the 1970s, of Bradshaw, Franco Harris, Mean Joe Greene, Lynn Swann, Jack Ham and many, many others fully restored. Every family has a father, mother, older sibling, cousin, aunt, uncle or grandparent who lived and died with those teams, and who continues to live and die with the current edition, itself only one year removed from a Super Bowl visit.

The Steelers are a true unifying force in the Pittsburgh community.

"There definitely is an expectation here," noted offensive guard Will Wolford, who had played on those four straight Super Bowl-losing Buffalo squads. "The city and the players are both *expected* to win the division and *expected* us to get back to the Super Bowl."

The Steelers had always been about defense (a true Parcells team, in other words), and so, too, was this team. The strength of the Steelers lay in such rugged customers on defense as linebackers Levin Kirkland and Chad Brown, and defensive backs Rod Woodson and Carnell Lake. The Steelers would eventually have to play on the road after a wild-card opener with Indianapolis, but so what? This was a battle-hardened group, worthy of anyone's deepest respect.

Entering the playoffs, no quarterback had thrown for 300 yards against the Steelers all year. One man, Baltimore's Bam Morris, had run for 100 yards against them, and his total was 100-even, not 101. And he needed 28 carries to do it. The next highest rushing totals surrendered by the Steelers were 77 and 69. In 16 games, there were only four runs of 15 or more yards against them. Oh, no, the Steeler defense was no myth. These were no PR totals; this was the reality of playing against the Pittsburgh Steelers.

Offense? Well, OK, the Steelers had their problems, even with Bettis running for all those yards. Tomczak may have ranked among the top 10 toughest QBs in the league, and he might also have ranked among the top five nicest and most sincere people, but he was not a quarterback who was going to strike fear in anyone's heart. The Steelers were having trouble scoring points in the late stages of the season. In the final four weeks of the season they had only been able to accumulate 62 points (17, 16, 15 and 14, so let no one say the offense, feeble though it was, hadn't been consistent). And Bettis, the primary offensive weapon, was coming into the play-offs with bad ankles (plural), not to mention a pulled groin.

Regardless, the Steelers oozed confidence. Their defense was what it was, and they had that championship taste in their mouths. The catch-phrase of the moment: "One for the thumb." Surely, you can figure *that* one out.

Any doubts that the Steelers were ready for the play-offs were distilled in the wild-card game against the fading Colts, who had gotten into the playoffs by the hair on their chinny-chin-chin, and who were too banged up to do much once they got there. Take away two plays, and there would absolutely have been no game. The two Indianapolis touchdowns in this game were both the result of interceptions, one of which was Tomczak's fault, and one of which wasn't. But two scores weren't going to be enough to hang in with Pittsburgh in this one. The final score at Three Rivers Stadium was 42-14, Steelers.

"And we're not done yet," growled Kirkland, the Pro Bowl-bound linebacker. "We still have a lot we can accomplish. I think the national audience saw that we're still the (AFC) champions, and that we will be the champs until someone beats us. We are the champions, and people will have to respect that, in some form or fashion."

The Colts had no choice but to respect them. Indianapolis finished with eight first downs (none rushing) and 41 yards on the ground. Bettis, bad ankles, pulled groin and all, ran for 102 yards. "I thrive on big games," he gushed. "When those lights go on, that's what I live for. That started at Notre Dame. We played a lot of big games."

Tomczak had come up with a big game, zipping a 30-yard bullet to wide receiver C.J. Johnson on the game's second play from scrimmage to get the fans into the game. He found himself yo-yo'd a bit in Pittsburgh's unique fashion, alternating to some degree with dynamic second-year quarterback/wide receiver Kordell Stewart, whom Steeler coach Bill Cowher liked to employ as a third-down and goal-line quarterback because of his great running ability. "He's Mr. Electricity and I'm the blue collar guy," shrugged Tomczak.

"Nothing was planned," said Cowher, answering questions concerning Stewart's most extended playing time at quarterback of the entire season. "It's a feel thing. There were some things Kordell did even I didn't know he had. I was enjoying the show myself."

Back in Boston, the game with Pittsburgh, the Patriots' first home playoff game since a 1978 loss to Houston (31-14), was being viewed on many levels. In addition to the team aspect, it was being regarded as a rite of passage game for Drew Bledsoe, who had come up with some very big games in the 1996 season, interspersed with some very poor ones. He was going to the Pro Bowl for the second time in his four-year career, but there were still many who felt he needed to come up with a big game against Pittsburgh in order to validate his greatness.

Among those not subscribing to that school of thought was his coach. As the season progressed, Parcells had grown more and more proprietary toward his kid QB. He may have been doing it out of both a sense of general loyalty and a sense of worry that if he didn't leap to Bledsoe's defense the latter might develop some sort of confidence problem, but the more likely reason he was so continually passionate about Bledsoe is that he generally liked him. It probably isn't necessary to go so far as to suggest that the kid was the son The Tuna never had, but Bledsoe did have many of the qualities a Parcells would want in an offspring.

Bledsoe was himself the son of a high school football coach, and unlike many who had grown up in that sort of environment, had come out of it as a refreshingly normal human being. His father, Mac Bledsoe, was more of a teacher/coach than a coach/teacher. Bledsoe was raised to think of himself as no better or worse than his siblings. He takes his job seriously, but not himself. Even better, he didn't come equipped with a stage father. Mac Bledsoe knows his football, but the last thing he would ever do in the world is presume to tell Bill Parcells what to do with his quarterback, even if it is his son. Small wonder that Mr. Bledsoe was welcomed to spend time on the Patriots' sideline any time he chose.

Parcells had developed Bledsoe. He was the only coach Bledsoe knew as a professional, and he was, quite obviously, pleased to be the architect of what was turning out to be a very nice professional career. He probably didn't want people putting down Bledsoe because he felt that to do so would be, in part, a reflection of *him*.

The Tuna would have none of this *Defining Opportunity* (words in an actual newspaper headline) stuff. "I told him," said Parcells, "'Don't worry about this big-game stuff, because you've won big games. You're gonna be judged by what your team accomplishes and whether you get them into the end zone. Nothing else. Those passing stats don't mean anything. It's what you did to let your team win.'

"Nobody ever brings up that 84-yard drive against Buffalo as a big play in the fourth quarter of a big game," continued The Tuna, "but that's exactly what it was. That was just as significant to me in his development than this other stuff of losing to those teams (i.e. Denver, Dallas, Washington)."

158

One other interesting aspect of this game would be the field. The Patriots had played their final home game against the Jets on December 8 (the day when Sam Gash went down for the count on the shameful playing surface) and in the meantime the entire field had been re-sodded, to the tune of $100,000, the expense borne by the National Football League itself. There was no guarantee the new sod would hold.

On the morning of Sunday, January 5, game day, Parcells awoke to see, well, not much. Fog had rolled in. Serious, San Francisco/London, ground-all-airplanes fog. Well, as the late, great, Gilda Radner said, "It's always something."

The game was scheduled for 12:30 p.m. EST, and the forecast wasn't good. The game was going to be played in deep, deep fog. Who was *that* going to favor? Stevie Wonder?

This was serious fog. NBC had arrived with about 70 kazillion (OK, 12) cameras at its disposal, and guess how many skilled director Andy Rosenberg got to use? Four. And they were lucky they could use that many. Rosenberg would later say, "The pictures were as good as we could get them. It was a constant balancing act between clarity and depth of view. The fog changed the entire game."

The time any major network director had been faced with anything comparable was back on December 31, 1988, when a similar fog had rolled off Lake Michigan onto the city of Chicago. Soldier Field abuts the lake. The Eagles and Bears haven't seen the football yet. In this case, the national TV audience never got one glimpse of the Foxboro Stadium scoreboard.

It was likewise questionable just exactly what the visiting Steelers saw of the Patriots. Writers from learned and respected journals from every corner of this great land of ours had to exercise great restraint, but in the end, few could resist. How could you not look at this almost ridiculously easy 28-3 Patriots' triumph and not put something down in that computer alluding to the Steelers "being in a fog" of some sort?

The awful truth that perhaps the Steelers shoulda stayed in bed materialized on the very first Patriots' play from scrimmage.

The Steelers had taken the opening kickoff and had gone nowhere. On Tomczak's first pass attempt, two things happened. One, he found himself staring at a half ton or so of angry beef. Two, Lawyer Milloy, the young safety Parcells was starting to love, was laying a serious hurt on Pittsburgh wide receiver Jamie Arnold.

Welcome to Foxboro, defending, or should we say, soon to be ex-champs.

The Patriots took over at their own 45. Nice field position. Bledsoe faded back and hit a streaking Terry Glenn (who had simply gone beep-beep past a startled Rod Woodson) on the right sideline for a 53-yard gain. Better field position. Martin, who would finish with 166 yards and three touchdowns, took it in, and the ballgame was over. With 59 minutes and 9 seconds left to play.

What a greeting. It was like a Rickey Henderson lead-off home run on the first pitch of a World Series game.

"Ray Perkins said we are not going to come out and be conservative," explained Glenn. "We're going to come out and show them we are not scared. We're going after them."

"Terry Glenn has speed," pointed out Dave Meggett, "but I know Woodson didn't know from watching film how fast Terry really is. You can't judge Terry's speed from game film...he's *really* fast."

The Patriots, led by Curtis Martin's 169 yards and three touchdowns, shredded the defending AFC champions' defense. (Photo©Tom Miller)

Soon it was 14-0 (a 34-yard Byars catch-and-run the drive's key play) and then it was 21-0 when Martin took a second-quarter handoff and made like Forest Gump. He didn't stop running until he reached the goal line, 78 yards away, but had it been necessary he could have run to Bledsoe's house in Walla Walla. It was a pitchout. Coates made a good block to spring him, Carnell Lake and Kirkland both missed him, and then it was hello, paydirt. "I think they had a blitz on," pointed out Parcells. "And when you hit one of those against that, there aren't many people left." Parcells added that when someone does what Martin did on that play it is known as "taking it to the house."

"That was probably my longest run ever," Martin said. "College, Pop Warner, *anything*."

The Tuna may very nearly have exhausted his ratio of pronouns, but not his enthusiasm for this game. Why, there was even a picture of him with a good-sized grin on his face plastered across the morning paper on the Day After.

The Patriots shredded the vaunted Steelers' defense for 346 yards. There might easily have been a lot more statistical fun to be had, but messrs. Parcells and Perkins called off the hounds early, placing Bledsoe into a conservative mode for most of the second half. But that didn't stop Martin, playing against his hometown team, from making another bid for the NFL's season highlight Hall of Fame film with a dazzling 23-yard touchdown run in the fourth quarter to complete the scoring. Anatomically speaking, a body isn't supposed to be able to do things Martin's did on this particular jaunt. No doubt the Steelers wanted to know why The Tuna hadn't been satisfied with Marion (One Yard and a Wisp of Dust) Butts.

It was such a thorough rout that Bledsoe got to watch the end of it with his Patriots' baseball hat perched on his head as longtime backup (and Bledsoe buddy) Scott Zolak took some precious snaps. 'Zo even managed to complete two out of three passes.

Pittsburgh's offense was nonexistent. Tomczak produced nothing (16-for-29, 110 yards). Slash Stewart was a pathetic 0-for-10. Bettis aggravated his groin injury but somehow managed 43 yards on sheer determination before he had to leave the game. Punter Josh Miller had plenty of air time. He was out there doing his thing nine times, including the first seven Pittsburgh possessions.

The Patriots shouldn't have needed any artificial stimuli in order to get ready for this game, but they managed to find it by adopting the great athletes' mantra of the '90s: "We don't get no respect." The Patriots were indeed the favorites (2½ points), and there certainly was enough local giddiness, but the players somehow decided they were being "disrespected."

"I don't want to take anything away from Pittsburgh," said McGinest. "but they didn't give us any respect. They were supposed to have this big defense. Slash this, Slash that..and Bettis. No one gave us a chance. We didn't want to talk to you guys (i.e. the media)."

"I try not to read the papers too much," added Ty Law. "but I happened to pick it up and they had a position-by-position on the defense. Pittsburgh pretty much beat us everywhere. We had a lot to prove out there. As the secondary, they talked a lot about Rod Woodson and Carnell Lake being Pro Bowlers. Parcells didn't have to say a word. I just picked that paper up and was ready to go. When someone tells you you're not going to do this, or not going to do that, of course that gives you extra motivation to go out and play."

The basic Pittsburgh take on this miserable afternoon in the fog: "I don't think we played a very good game," said coach Cowher, who lamented the fact that the Patriots had broken three big plays against his defense. "You know, there's a very fine line between the top teams in this business, and it often comes down to a game of momentum — and they got it."

January 12 vs. Jacksonville
New England 20, Jacksonville 6

The traditional role of an expansion team in any sport is to dispense the entry fee checks to the senior partners of the firm and then go sit down in a corner somewhere and prepare to accept your beatings. These whippings should last anywhere from five to 25 years. Meanwhile, you are supposed to express frequent public thanks to the league fathers for allowing you the privilege of serving as a doormat for the established teams in the league.

Free agency has changed all that.

With free agency, expansion teams can win games much more quickly than they could in the old days. The Colorado Rockies made the baseball playoffs in the third year of their existence, and their first, as luck would have it, in their snaking new cash cow of a home field. The Florida Panthers didn't need much time to reach hockey's Stanley Cup Finals. And then along came the Carolina Panthers and the Jacksonville Jaguars of the National Football League.

What do you think the odds would have been on a preseason parlay calling for the second-year Panthers and Jaguars each playing for a conference championship on the second Sunday of January? 100,000 to 1? A million to 1? Incalculable to 1?

But this virtually incomprehensible daily double came home in 1997. The defensive-minded Carolina Panthers of Dom Capers and the breathtaking Jacksonville Jaguars quarterbacked by the dynamic Mark Brunell and coached by Tom Coughlin did what no one on earth had foreseen back in August. Each had not only made the playoffs in its second year, but each had also reached the finals of its respective conference. Each was one game away from the Super Bowl.

Savvy management and the astute personnel selections of Bill Polian in Carolina and Coughlin himself in Jacksonville had produced quality teams. But it must be pointed out that these clubs were also gifted with the most generous drafting possibilities ever given to expansion teams in the history of American professional sport. The norm is for leagues to stifle newcomers in the draft arena, but the NFL reversed that policy in regard to the Panthers and Jaguars. A coin flip had determined that Carolina would receive the first pick of the 1995 draft and Jacksonville would pick second. The Panthers would then select first in odd-numbered rounds and the Jaguars would pick first in even-numbered rounds.

But there was more. The official policy statement read as follows: "The two expansion teams will each receive one extra pick, for a total of 14 picks. In the 1996 college draft, the two teams will receive one extra choice after each of their original picks in rounds three through five, and two extra picks in the sixth and seventh rounds for a total of 14 picks. The additional picks will fall 15 selections after the team's original choice in the sixth and seventh rounds."

Whew!

What this all means was that with any kind of sagacious drafting, the expansion teams could get their hands on a great deal of young talent. Football, unlike baseball or hockey, and surely unlike basketball, values non-first-round draft picks. It takes a lot of warm bodies to stock the roster of a football team. This is a sport where second- and third-round picks are valued commodities in trades. It is a sport where a sixth- or seventh-round selection results in a valued member of a special teams unit. And here these new clubs were going to receive 14 players in seven rounds without forfeiting anything in return. Not bad, not bad at all.

Contrast this approach to the NBA's most recent expansion. The World's Greatest Basketball League has denied the expansions access to the first pick in the draft for three years! The Vancouver Canucks or Toronto Raptors could have gone 0-82 and still not gotten a crack at Tim Duncan.

The NFL has long been regarded as a great monument to socialism, and here was yet another example of the league's egalitarian personality at work. But the people in charge still had to make good decisions. Football is indeed like its basketball, baseball and hockey brethren in that in the end it all comes down to opinion. There are damned few legitimate sure things in any sport. No one is a guaranteed success, if only because of injury. Pervis Ellison was the number one pick in an NBA draft. Tony Mandarich was the number two pick in an NFL draft. And if you want to talk about bad luck, how about the New York Yankees throwing more than a million dollars at a South Carolina high school pitching prospect named Brien Taylor, only to see him ruin his career by rushing to the aid of his brother during an off-season altercation, and, in so doing, messing up his left (or throwing) shoulder, apparently beyond repair.

Neither the Panthers nor the Jaguars made too many serious personnel mistakes. Each benefitted from free agency. The Panthers were able to establish instant credibility on defense in 1995. Among their conquests were the New England Patriots, whom they upended by a 20-17 score in overtime. This game practically pushed Patriots fans over the edge. It dropped the team record to 2-6 and it may very well have been a 1995 low point. As Parcells trudged off the field that day, a leather-lung sort jumped up in the end zone and began to vent. "Hey, Bill," he yelled, "we need a puntah, we need a wide receivah and we need an awffensive coordinatah!"

That was a pretty sound assessment, as it turned out. The fan got two out of his three wishes. He got Tom Tupa to kick and he got Terry Glenn to catch the ball. He didn't get rid of Ray Perkins, but after watching his team average 30-plus points a game for a good portion of the season, the fan might have rescinded druther number three.

The Patriots knew all about the Jacksonville Jaguars. This was the "Hail Mary" team, remember? But at no point during the months of November and December did the Patriots ever think they would wind up playing the Jaguars again. They had every reason to believe they had placed the Jaguars in the rear view mirror.

After losing to the Cincinnati Bengals in Week 9 the Jags had fallen to 3-6, the same record the 1994 Patriots had tumbled to before beginning their turnaround. Then, mercifully, came the Bye Week. Coach Coughlin took advantage of the situation to do some retooling, and when Week 10 came for the Jaguars they were a different team. They beat Baltimore. They lost to Pittsburgh the following week, and then they really acquired some momentum. They knocked off Baltimore again (in overtime), and then Cincinnati, Houston and Atlanta fell.

That brought them to the final game of the season. They were 8-7. They needed a victory over Atlanta in order to make the playoffs, but with little time left the cause looked hopeless. They led the Falcons, 19-17, 'tis true, but now Morton Andersen was lining up for a 30-yard field goal that would win the game. Win or lose, there would be no time left. The last time Morton Andersen had missed a field goal from that distance was in 1989, when he was a member of the New Orleans Saints, and when, conceivably, he might have been out closing down Bourbon Street the night before — who knows?

Let Jacksonville season ticket holder Tom Correia tell the story. "To be honest," he reported, "I walked out. I thought, 'Morton Andersen, he's one of the greatest place-kickers ever.' A guy next to me had a radio, and he started screaming, 'He missed it!' And then it started to get crazy."

Did it ever.

"I was in here working," said Mike Callahan, the kitchen manager of "Sneakers," a popular sports bar/restaurant, "and I knew the guy hadn't missed one since '89, and when it happened, I don't think people really *knew* what happened. There was like a 10-second delay in here before the place exploded."

The Jaguars were now in the playoffs on a "What-the-hell" basis. That was a goal enough in itself. But a funny thing happened on the way to the golf course. The Jaguars went to Buffalo and kicked their butts. Mark Brunell passed and Mark Brunell ran and Natrone Means, the official Reclamation Project of the National Football League, ran and mammoth offensive tackle Tony Boselli (6-7, 325 or so) stifled legendary All-Pro end and AFC Defensive Player of the Year Bruce Smith and the Jaguars knocked off the Bills in Rich Stadium.

They were starting to get everyone's attention. People were now aware that Brunell, a one-time backup to Brett Favre in Green Bay whom the Jags had acquired in a clever trade for a pair of fifth-round picks, had thrown for 4,367 yards and 19 touchdowns when most of the outside world was looking elsewhere. People were now aware that Means, a former San Diego star who had been dumped amid charges of poor conditioning and an even poorer attitude, had just ripped apart the proud Bills for 175 yards.

They really started paying attention when Means came out against Denver, in Denver, and ran all over the haughty Broncos for 140 more yards the following week. The squat (5-10, 240 pounds) running back was like some kind of football Born-Again, determined to demonstrate to a doubting public that he was once again one of the premier running backs in captivity.

While all this was going on, Jacksonville fans, more accustomed to rooting home the University of Florida Gators, were beginning to lose their hearts to the Jaguars. When the team flew home after defeating Denver, more than 40,000 people trooped into their home stadium for an impromptu postmidnight rally.

As the Patriots-Jaguars game approached, people couldn't get enough out of the fact that the Parcells-Coughlin coaching matchup was one of teacher vs. pupil. Coughlin and Parcells went back a long way. Coughlin had been an assistant with Parcells during the glory days in New York. He accepted the job as head coach of Boston College after the 1990 season and his first official act was to make four recruiting calls from the locker room of a Super Bowl winner. He got all four players, and he turned around the Boston College program with his aggressive, no-nonsense approach to football.

The Jaguars made him one of those offers he just couldn't refuse, and off he went to run the expansion team. He was, and is, the final word on all matters football in that town, and he has done nothing to abuse that trust.

Parcells did nothing to disguise his love and admiration for his old friend, and Coughlin did likewise. But each man tried to downplay the relationship, at least insofar as it would have any bearing on the upcoming game. "Our friendship will go far beyond this game," Coughlin said. "It's not going to matter on Sunday."

Coughlin had such an image as a disciplinarian that he had almost become a caricature of himself. There was a seemingly endless list of dos and don'ts, and there was a lot of grumbling among the players — in the beginning. But once they learned that he had a vast knowledge of football, and that everything he did had a logical purpose, the intelligent players simmered down. The others moved on, and they were not missed.

The Patriots' major concerns were stopping Brunell from dictating the tempo and flow of the game and preventing Means from doing unto them as he had done to Buffalo and Denver (315 yards combined). Means was the same kind of runner as Jerome Bettis, but unlike the battered Pittsburgh ace, he was coming into the AFC title game with fresh legs.

This time there was no fog. The weather was no factor. It was cold (25 or so) by the kickoff time (4 p.m. EST), but it was New England wintry weather and nothing more. People such as Parcells and John Madden would have declared it to be perfect playoff weather. Andy Rosenberg had no problems utilizing any camera he liked. That is, until the lights went out.

Hey, this was New England. The lights had once gone out in Boston Garden during a Stanley Cup Finals game with Edmonton. The lights had gone out in the new Fleet Center in a Celtics-Toronto game 31 days earlier. And now, at 4:53 p.m., with 7:23 remaining in the first half of the AFC title game at 26-year old Foxboro Stadium, the lights went out once again, just as the Patriots, already leading 7-3, were lining up for a Vinatieri field goal from the Jacksonville 12.

Given the amount of stadium talk in the air, many people joked that Bob Kraft had brazenly picked this dramatic forum to demonstrate just how badly, and how quickly, he needed a new venue for his team. But the actual source of the blackout had nothing whatsoever to do with Foxboro Stadium or the New England Patriots. The story was that a quarter-inch piece of steel twine some 12-15 inches long had burned out. The whole area had been plunged into darkness. Three repairmen from Massachusetts Electric replaced the fuse. The delay was a manageable 11 minutes.

Vinatieri kicked his 29-yard field goal, and life went on.

This was nothing like the Pittsburgh game. Jacksonville made a huge early boo-boo, but the Jaguars never lost control of the game as Pittsburgh had.

The Patriots did not kick Jacksonville's butt. They beat them by a 20-6 score to earn their second Super Bowl berth, and their first in 11 years, but they had to keep playing until the final 2½ minutes, or until Jets expatriate Otis Smith came up with a Jacksonville fumble and returned it 47 yards for what can be called the ultra-clinching touchdown.

Breaks, especially early ones, can be crucial in a game of this magnitude, and there was a colossal one in the first two minutes. The Jaguars had just come out with a wimpy 1-2-3-nothing after taking the opening kickoff, and rookie punter Bryan Barker was now about to execute the "kick" part when a very bad thing happened to Jags. There was a high snap from center. It was high, but

Shawn Jefferson made four catches for 91 yards, including a reception on a picture-perfect pass play from Bledsoe that led to a field goal just before halftime. (Photo©Tom Miller)

not *too* high, and certainly it was not sufficiently high to prevent any experienced kicker from catching the ball and getting off a punt, however wobbly.

Tom Tupa, for example, would have kicked the ball away — no problem. But young Mr. Barker panicked. He decided he couldn't get the punt off, and he wound up being tackled by the ubiquitous Larry Whigham at the Jacksonville one-yard line. Bledsoe sent Martin into the end zone. The Patriots would never trail. They would never dominate, but they would never trail.

This one turned out to be a defensive triumph. Brunell, who had tormented the Patriots for 422 yards in the first game and who had found himself being compared to the great Steve Young after taking apart both Buffalo and Denver, was held in check by the aroused, inspired, underrated Patriots defense. He finished at 20-for-38 for a very liveable 190 yards. He was intercepted twice.

Means was never a factor, either. Somewhere along the way he sustained a sprained right ankle. He finished with 43 yards, and, to his credit, he refused to alibi. "My foot got rolled, kind of sprained on the outside, like it was about to explode," he said. "You try to work through it, but, no excuses, they really played great defense all day long."

Offense was simply not the story for the Patriots, although there was one very big play late in the half. The situation: A fourth-and-three from the Jacksonville 45 with 29 seconds left in the half. Parcells, predictably, went for it. But this time he *really* went for it. Bledsoe flung one up the far left sideline for a streaking Shawn Jefferson (four catches, 91 yards). The ball could not have been better thrown had he simply run down there and handed it to Jefferson. He hit the wide receiver in stride, and with enough spacing between his feet and the sideline to eliminate the need for any fancy stepping in order to remain inbounds. That 38-yard completion set up a confidence-building Vinatieri field goal.

Parcells was proud of the Bledsoe-Jefferson collaboration. "We've practiced that play for three years for just that occasion," he confided. "Excuse me, we've practiced it for *four* years. No timeouts, 15 seconds to go, we need

20 or 30 yards. What will we do? We've only run it one other time in the four years I've been here, and it was overthrown. We know we can't get tackled inbounds. We just happened to catch it."

But all the other notable Patriots' plays in this game featured the defenders. Marty Moore, a valued special teamer, produced a score by separating Jacksonville punt returner Chris Hudson from the football, leading to a Mike Bartrum recovery and another Vinatieri field goal (10-3).

Late in the game, the Patriots came up with two more monster defensive plays. Brunell led his team on a fourth-quarter march, the drive beginning on the Jacksonville 37 and continuing all the way to the Patriots' five. The lead at the time was only 13-6.

On second down Brunell faded back and for an instant he was sure he had located an unguarded Derek Brown. But Willie Clay stepped in and made what he called "the biggest interception of my life."

"It would have been nice to run it back 100 yards," said the man known throughout New England, now and forever, as "Big Play."

"I don't think he saw me coming, or else he wouldn't have thrown it," Clay continued. "It was just the right read. I saw him looking to my side."

But the game wasn't over yet. The Patriots' offense generated nothing more than a quick three-and-out, and the Jags had the ball back at their own 42. That's when Chris Slade came charging in to nail backup running back James Stewart (subbing for the ailing Means) from the ball. Otis Smith scooped it up and he ran it 47 yards into the end zone to put the game away.

"I was just coming up to make the tackle," said Smith. "One of my teammates came up from behind and

Otis Smith (45) grabs the ball after a fumble by Jacksonville's James Stewart. Smith returned the ball for a touchdown to assure the Patriots of a 20-7 victory. (Photo©Tom Miller)

stripped it, and I just ran as fast as I could. I can't tell you how exciting it is to make a play like this in a game as big as this."

As time wound down, Parcells got to savor the moment. These are the precious seconds he so often talks about, when he can look at the happy faces of the players who have given him so much. All professional football seasons begin in the sweltering heat of summer with frightful two-a-day sessions, and for most teams all seasons end in the brutal winter cold. In between the team has any number of ups and downs, of false starts and indecisive moments. There are days when any football player hates his coach, his teammates and perhaps even himself. It is a very, very tough, demanding and curious way to make a living, and the rewards are fleeting. Parcells articulates this as well as any man alive, and he appreciates it *more* than any man alive.

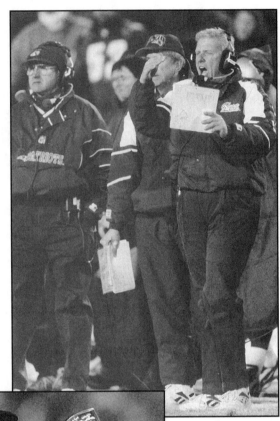

Bill Parcells watches as his team wins the AFC championship. (Photo©Tom Miller)

Willie McGinest took former USC teammate Tony Boselli to school in the AFC championship game, then showed off the newly won trophy. (Photo©Tom Miller)

"I see the faces on these players," he said. "I remember the faces on the players I had before who went and how happy they were. That's the priceless thing in this business. Those faces are the faces you remember. You see those kids and there is a bond there on days like that which never leaves."

And now he was ready to pay public tribute to those players. "I'm thankful to these players who have given me everything I've asked for throughout the year," he said. "They played like they showed me all throughout the year that we had a chance."

It was moments like this, and statements like these, which would come back to haunt Parcells a month later when he found it amazingly easy to say good-bye to those faces, and those players, the people he had spent weeks and months professing to love.

But all that was in the future. This was a totally happy day in the life of Bill Parcells and his players. His moment of truth came in the final seconds when Chris Slade, abetted by his close friend Willie McGinest, sneaked up behind the mentor to dump the ceremonial Gatorade on Bill Parcells. Truth be told, it was less than a perfect dump. "I wish I'd gotten it on top of his head," Slade confessed, "but I missed." Ah, well, the side of the head and the shoulder were just going to have to do, Chris.

Among the subplots in this game was a battle between ex-USC mates Boselli and McGinest. There had been much publicity attached to Boselli's domination of Bruce Smith in the Buffalo game, but in this confrontation the players assumed their old college roles. That is to say, McGinest was the teacher and Boselli was the pupil. McGinest was just too quick and resourceful for Boselli, who, after all, was only in his second professional season.

"I came out in my mind that I was going to do the best I could," confided McGinest. "I've been playing with him for almost five years. I knew what he had. He pretty much knew what I had. I just stayed focused and calm. I took what he gave me."

McGinest's reasoned, professional attitude was emblematic of a superb overall team defensive performance. After all The Tuna's worries earlier in the season about the quality of his defense, in this most important game of the season the unit which had refused to buckle and which carried the team across the finish line (with help, as usual, from the special teams) was the defense. That would have been difficult to believe back about the time of Denver 34, New England 8.

And many of the players admitted that the Denver debacle was the best thing that had ever happened to them. "

"Denver?" said Lawyer Milloy. "Embarrassing. I'm not saying everybody expected us to *beat* Denver that day, but we just didn't show up. We all knew how bad we had been."

"That Denver game," added Ted Johnson, "humbled us. It knocked us off the little pedestal we thought we were on and brought us back to earth real quick. From that point on, we've made a concerted effort to get things done. Since then, we've been making big plays."

Winning via defense, and not via some Shootout at the OK Corral, put a spring in The Tuna's step. He was moved to rehash one of his favorite themes.

"We spoke a lot this season about whether we were gonna be club fighters or champions," he said. "Club fighters are of a certain mentality. They work hard, but they don't aspire to anything. For a while, this organization had that mentality. But I told the team after the game they can't call us club fighters anymore."

Patriots
Fever

Boston had officially become a football town. Some people were trying to say that the feeling in December 1985 and January 1986, the period of time in which the Patriots had won three road games in order to become AFC champions and earn their first trip to the Super Bowl, was as fanatical, but that was a very foolish notion, if for no other reason than in the first instance there was no Tuna in Boston, and the clear motto in January of 1997 was "In Tuna We Trust."

Patriots fever had engulfed everyone, and why not? The Celtics and Bruins were both embarrassments and eyesores. It was too early to become fixated on the Red Sox. Anyone interested in sports who happened to live in Greater Boston had little recourse but to follow the New England Patriots, who were now on their way to a Super Bowl date with the Green Bay Packers.

How crazy was it? Well, consider that on the evening of January 12, the same day on which the Patriots had defeated the Jaguars to become champions of the AFC, a 7-pound, 6-ounce baby boy was born to Tina and Donald Linscott in Anna Jacques Hospital in Newburyport, Massachusetts, a coastal town located about 35 miles northeast of Boston.

And what did they name this child? How about Curtis Martin Linscott?

"She is not a football fan, but I'm working on it," said Donald Linscott. "But we were trying for months to come up with a name and couldn't. One day, two months ago, I was watching a game and she heard the name Curtis Martin. She said, 'Hmmm, I like that name.' Of course, I didn't fight her."

Another name on everyone's lips in the immediate aftermath of the AFC title game was Sam Gash. The classy fullback had not been able to play since the second Jets' game, but everyone wanted to talk with him because right after the game, and on national television, Bill Parcells had him paid a great tribute, telling Gash that he was missed and could not be replaced.

"It was just something that came into my head when I got the microphone," Parcells explained. "Sam is one of the original six who were here when I got here. He's been at every off-season workout, every practice and every game until he got hurt. That makes him different. It just crossed my mind when I got up there. I knew he had just been operated on and was probably watching in the hospital. I wanted him to know he was important to us."

Sam Gash heard his tribute from The Tuna while lying in his bed at Massachusetts General Hospital in Boston. It was, as you might expect, just about the last thing he was expecting to hear less than 10 minutes after the conclusion of the AFC title game. "It caught me as much by surprise as anyone," he later admitted. "I kind of got choked up, and when I called my wife, she was crying. I'm not that emotional about things. But it just felt great to have him mention my name, because he's a great coach, and because I respect him so much."

The Tuna even found something good to say about the owner he was fighting with behind the scenes. "You need good players, and you need to be in the right situation," he said, "and you've got to have a good support system. If you don't have that, you can't succeed in this business. I've been very fortunate."

That's not what he'd be saying a month later, but the owner himself wasn't being very forthcoming on the subject of his relations with Bill Parcells, either. But on the day after coaching his team to the AFC title The Tuna was in a very accommodating mood. "I hope we get this championship for the people of New England," he said. "I really do."

Many of the queries concerned the comparison and/ or differences between getting to the Super Bowl with the Giants and returning with this Patriots team. For the most part, he said, there is no difference.

"You have to understand there is no feeling like standing in that tunnel at the Super Bowl waiting to take the field," he said. "There is nothing like it. I remember being in Pasadena (1987), and I know who was standing beside me, and who was where, and it was the same thing in Tampa Bay (1991). There is just no feeling like it."

He would have no way of knowing how the game would turn out of course, but one thing he knew was just how well he had coached this year. He was pleased to say he had done a better job than in 1995.

"I always judge myself the same way," he explained. "Did I get this team to play to its potential? If the answer

Bill Parcells got a great deal of satisfaction from the 1996 Patriots. (Photo©Tom Miller)

is yes, I don't care what anybody thinks. If I know in my heart that my team has played as well as it can, then I'm happy; I've done a good job. I felt like I failed last year. The year before, we overachieved a little. But we should have been at least 8-8 last year."

"This year's team did what it should. At 0-2 I still thought we'd be all right. At 3-3 I knew it would come down to how well we did in those four division games. They were the turning point of the season. I thought that if we got through those, we'd have a good chance to go down fighting."

The Tuna seized this session as an opportunity to put in a word for his quarterback, who had not been putting up big numbers in the playoffs. "You wonder why coaches and players sometimes have a problem with the media," he said. "The important question is 'Where is his team?' There is an old saying, 'You judge a trapper by his furs.' Well, Drew is starting to get a few of those furs."

The Tuna was not the only person feeling an immense amount of satisfaction. Veteran tackle Bruce Armstrong was in his 10th year without a whole lot to show for his career other than a few Pro Bowl assignments and some scars. A year earlier he had come away believing that the Patriots had squandered some talent. He had made the following declaration: "I want 13-3, the division championship, home-field advantage in the playoffs and then I want the Super Bowl. I'm not worried about money. I'm not worried about how I'm perceived around the league. I just want to win."

How's that? It was 11-5, not 13-3, but the rest had all come true. This season had vindicated everything Armstrong had always believed about the game. His experience had taught him that winning was the product of something more than raw talent. He was starting to worry that he would wind up in retirement before ever getting a chance to play on a team that would ever get, you know, *it*.

"It's making them (ie. the younger players) understand that everything they do affects someone else," he pointed out. "It's things like showing up on time for meetings and wearing the proper equipment. You have to explain that it's important to earn the respect of your teammates. It's not a matter of turning out paper soldiers. We're not robots out there. We've got a lot of different personalities on this team. It's a matter of getting everyone pointed in the same direction on the field."

And that, of course, is what Bill Parcells specializes in doing. He may have his equals — and the word "may" is a polite supposition — but he most definitely has no superiors in the art of starting off with a group of players in the heat of July and molding them into a viable unit capable of playing anyone by December. He can't exactly make chicken salad out of chicken excrement; no one can. He needed a talent infusion in order to implement some of his policies. But once he got that talent, he and his staff knew what to do with it.

Four years in New England had culminated in that victory over Jacksonville. But the job was not yet done. The Tuna had become legendary not just because his teams in New York had twice gone to the Super Bowl. He had become a legend because he had twice gone to the Super Bowl and had come away with the winner's ring. But win or lose, there was a special thrill attached to being involved in the Super Bowl. "It's a euphoria," he said. "Maybe everybody isn't affected that way, but that's the way it is for me. I'm not being nostalgic, but when I saw those faces on my players Sunday I saw the same faces of those Giants players with the same look. It's almost like they were blended together."

For Bill Parcells, there was nothing more ironic than the fact in this return trip to the Super Bowl his team would be meeting Green Bay. For Green Bay's general manager was Ron Wolf, who just happened to be as good a friend as Bill Parcells has in the business.

It was fascinating to hear Bill Parcells, Mr. Self-Confident, talk about Ron Wolf. In every other football context, The Tuna invariably projects the aura of a man who has all the answers, but Ron Wolf turns out to be someone Bill Parcells actually looks up to. And he isn't even dead!

The Tuna normally lives a monastic existence on the road. He has a policy of never going out of the hotel, but he broke his rule in August in order to have dinner with Ron Wolf in Green Bay the night before that opening exhibition in August. The Tuna said that he studies Ron Wolf's roster moves in the hopes not only of finding a player, but of learning something. How about that?

Bill Parcells and Ron Wolf are neighbors during the off-season in Jupiter, Florida. The Tuna said that the two often sit around and discuss their respective wish lists, bouncing ideas back and forth with each other. And now they were each going to the Super Bowl.

"We'd just sit around and say, 'I need to get this,' or 'I need to get that,'" said Parcells. "It would just be good January football talk."

This year there would be no Florida commiserations. Their teams would meet for the championship of the known football world at 6:18 p.m. EST on the final Sunday of January 1997.

The Packers had paid all the requisite dues. They had been creeping close to the NFC title for three years, but an inability to defeat Dallas at Dallas would get in the way. Wolf had been assembling the pieces for years, and in Mike Holmgren, a one-time San Francisco offensive coordinator, he had a coach who could get the job done.

The Packers had been the best team in the league from start to finish. The only dip came at a time the team was battling injury. They finished at 13-3, but there had been a real chance to go 15-1. They clearly had the best offense-defense balance in the league, and they also had killer special teams, particularly with return teams anchored by the exciting Desmond Howard.

"We're going to have to play well to contain these guys," said Parcells.

There was no getting around it: Green Bay was a very formidable team. Not since Miami 25 years earlier had a team finished a season by scoring the most points while allowing the fewest. Though the public, and even some of the press, appeared fixated on league MVP Brett Favre and how many points (450) the Packers had rung up, Parcells thought that the scoring total told him just how good the defense was. "In order to score that many points," he reasoned, "you need the ball a lot. There must have been a lot of three-and-outs."

The Tuna was doing his best to keep every public conversation focused on pure football and the upcoming Super Bowl, and away from the topic most everyone wanted to discuss; namely, his personal future. Both he and Kraft would continue to insist that nothing had been decided, that they would sit down at the conclusion of the season and see where matters stood. But we would all learn later on that a great deal was happening, and that Parcells and Kraft were just another married couple ravaged by "irreconcilable differences."

The story would never go away, and it would erupt with a vengeance at the Super Bowl. But for the moment, both men were trying desperately to put a happy public face on the situation. The team deserved no less, and so did the public.

Next Stop, New Orleans

New Orleans, huh?

The Crescent City is always the best possible place for any sporting event. That is, of course, unless you have something against fun. Having a Super Bowl or a Final Four or some such thing is always the best possible reward for a fan who has latched onto a team.

But New Orleans conjured up some bad memories for Patriots fans. For New Orleans also happened to be the site of the Pats' one and only previous trip to the Super Bowl. To say the game was ugly from a Patriots' standpoint would be to suggest that it all went downhill for passengers on the Titanic after the ship ran into the iceberg.

It was the Patriots' misfortune on that day in 1986 to run into one of the best one-season teams that has ever performed in the National Football League. It was their further misfortune to run into the Chicago Bears on what might have been their best day of the season. The 46-10 final might not have been the worst statistical mismatch in the history of the Super Bowl (the 49ers would wallop the Broncos by a 55-10 count five years later), but in terms of artistic devastation and evidence of complete superiority, it has had no equal in the 31-year history of America's most-watched sporting event.

Talk about bubble-bursting...The Patriots were riding a sensational wave, having just done something no one has ever done, before or since. That team was the only NFL club ever to get to the Super Bowl by winning three consecutive road games. The Patriots earned their way to New Orleans by eliminating the Jets, the Raiders and the Dolphins. Only one other team, the 1980-81 Oakland Raiders, has ever reached the Super Bowl from the vantage point of a wild-card team and they didn't have to play all their pre-Super Bowl games on the road.

Fans were whipped up, and, while the Bears were clear favorites, there was every expectation in New England that the Patriots would give a good accounting of themselves. The Patriots actually led, 3-0, on an early Tony Franklin 36-yard field goal. Lawrence McGrew had pounced on a Chicago fumble at the Bears' 19 and it led to the quickest first-quarter score in Super Bowl history. And then, oh wow, *Le Deluge*...

Before this carnage was indelibly inked into the record books, the Bears had sacked Patriots quarterbacks Tony Eason and Steve Grogan a Super Bowl record seven times, and had held the Patriots to an almost ridiculous Super Bowl record of seven (7) yards on the ground. The Bears led 23-3 at the half and a totally embarrassing 44-3 after three periods. Quarterback Jim McMahon (12 of 20, 256 yards and two rushing touchdowns) cooly directed the Chicago attack, but the real story of the game was the suffocating Chicago defense, a unit many believe was the best of all time.

Some of the Patriots players will still tell you it was the worst day of their lives, and that they become embarrassed all over again each time they think about it.

Amazingly, the tenor of the Super Bowl visit got even worse, when, within a day or so of the game, it was revealed that several members of the Patriots had been dabbling (to say the least) in drugs. This miniscandal further besmirched the Super Bowl jaunt. It was almost as if those three glorious victories over New York, Los Angeles and Miami had never taken place.

So New Orleans didn't conjure up the best of memories for everyone in New England.

But it was, of course, a new Patriots organization. That trip to the Super Bowl was three owners ago. The team had been passed on by Billy Sullivan to Victor ("I Bought The Company") Kiam, to James Busch Orthwein, and now to Bob Kraft, who was gushing all over the place about just how wonderful all this was for his beloved fans (whom he had begun to call his "shareholders").

Kraft had rather serious and weighty matters of state sitting squarely on his head. First, there was this messy issue of his coach and their tattered partnership, a sordid tale which was a daily press nightmare for him. Secondly, there was the matter of a new stadium. In the middle of all this, Kraft was determined to enjoy himself in his position as owner of the new AFC champions.

This was, after all, why he had bought the team. Owning the Patriots was a true fantasy for a man who had long held title to tickets in section 217, row 23, seats 1 through 6. "I remember him coming home with those tickets," said son Jonathan, now a team vice president. "He was so excited, and so were we." The year was 1971, the first season the team moved into Foxboro Stadium. Kraft still thought of himself as a fan first, however self-delusionary that was in his current capacity.

Kraft knew the sad Patriots' Super Bowl history, but he had every confidence there would be no repeat of the Bears' fiasco. That put him in alignment with just about every facet of the Patriots' community, because there was no reason to think that a team with players such as Bledsoe, Coates, Glenn, Martin, McGinest and Byars couldn't play with the Green Bay Packers.

That opinion was not widely held outside of New England. The early Las Vegas line for the 1997 Super Bowl was 14 points.

In reality, it should have been seven or eight. The Packers looked to be a touchdown better, on paper. Throw in a couple or three more points for the NFC Super Bowl dominance (no AFC team had won since the Los Angeles Raiders had defeated the Washington Redskins in 1983) and a few more for the public's romantic attachment to the very *idea* of the Green Bay Packers, and there you have a 14-point line.

The Tuna wasn't interested in betting lines. The Patriots could have been 34-point underdogs or 40-point favorites, for all it mattered to him. He had very real concerns, things such as an MVP quarterback in Brett Favre, a player he had liked for his feistiness dating back to the kid's collegiate days; a killer defensive end in perennial All-Pro Reggie White ("I don't have to be educated to know what he's all about") and a game-breaking specialist in Desmond Howard, the centerpiece of Green Bay's return teams. Being a man who fancied himself as a special teams aficionado, Parcells was very concerned about Howard's potential to take a close game and make it Green Bay property. "I think Desmond Howard has ignited the Green Bay Packers as much as any player on the team, except for Brett Favre," he declared.

Parcells never tires of waxing eloquent on the subject of special teams. "It's 20 or 30 plays a game," he pointed out. "You're talking about a tremendous variance in field position. In this game, you're trying to advance the ball, and you're trying to keep them from doing it. It's what this game is all about."

He puts great care in selecting special teams players, and when he finds someone who has the knack he's looking for, he really embraces that player. One such performer was Larry Whigham. "He's just a very good athlete," Parcells explained. "He's got size and speed. And now he's experienced. He's flexible. He knows how to play his roles."

Marty Moore, who had come into the NFL bearing the lighthearted tag of "Mr. Irrelevant" after being the very last man chosen in the 1994 draft, was another such player. "A lot of these guys are never going to be stars," Parcells said. "Take Marty Moore. He'll probably never be a starter (at linebacker), but he is very valuable on special teams. He's reliable. He never misses a practice. You can count on him. A coach is probably always going to look for a better player to do his job, but he's not going to find one. Then all of a sudden the guy has a 10-year career. You can bring in a rookie and say, 'Beat him out,' and that kid is going to have his hands full."

Parcells said that he wasn't going to be an ogre at the Super Bowl. He wasn't expecting his team to become Trappists down there in the Big Easy. There would be no curfew the first few nights, and he didn't expect anyone to be abusing the privilege. "I know what they're supposed to look like at 8:30 in the morning," is the way he put it. He was very confident there would be no off-the-field problems, because, as he had pointed out to the local media on numerous occasions, it had proven to be a trustworthy group over the long haul. "There have been very few discipline problems," he declared.

The team even got a rah-rah sendoff to New Orleans in the form of a rally at City Hall Plaza. An estimated 15,000 people braved frigid mid-January temperatures to wish the team well. The fans cheered everyone but Boston mayor Thomas Menino, who was viewed by the rabble as a Luddite who didn't understand the importance of the downtown stadium Bob Kraft and Governor Bill Weld were pushing. Hizzoner was wounded by the hostile reception. "I've supported the Patriots for a long time," he wailed. "I remember watching them play at Fenway Park. How many of these people go all the way back to Fenway Park?"

Everything was fine when Parcells and the team arrived in New Orleans. The Tuna liked the hotel. The Tuna liked the security arrangement. The Tuna liked the setup of the meeting rooms. The Tuna lavished praise on Danny Kraft, another of the owner's sons. Danny, listed on the team masthead as the Vice President of Marketing and Sales, had been dispatched as the advance man back when getting to the Super Bowl was merely a hope. Danny had done a very good job of making all the key arrangements, he said. So everyone knew that Parcells at least believed that his owner had done *something* right in his life.

Everything was fine — until the next morning. That's because on Monday, January 20, Inauguration Day, a story appeared in the *Boston Globe* which stirred the pot and which became a huge *cause celebre*.

The story, written by the *Globe's* legendary Will McDonough, carried a simple enough headline: *Parcells Won't Return*. A prophetic subhead said, simply: *Controversy Looms*.

No kidding.

Was this story really full of, as they say, "new" news? Didn't everyone already assume that Parcells would not be coming back to New England and that he was heading to the Jets (who had yet to interview a soul for the head coaching job left behind by Rich Kotite)? Well, sure, but this somehow made it quasi-official, because it was written by McDonough, who was not merely a well-known, well-respected and ever much-feared journalist, but who was also a close personal friend of one Duane Charles (Bill) Parcells.

The story contained no direct quotes from anyone on the subject of Parcells' plans, but it did include quotes from Robert Fraley, the agent for Bill Parcells. The automatic assumptions of those writers and broadcasters capable of adding up a couple of journalistic twos and arriving at the number four were a) Fraley had been the source of the article and b) Fraley would not have said anything to McDonough at this particular point in time without the express permission of his client, Bill Parcells.

If that were the case, why would Parcells choose the beginning of Super Bowl week to drop the official bomb? A little background is necessary. On the morning of the AFC title game, Parcells had awakened to see a story written by Kevin Mannix in the *Boston Herald*, the gist of which was that in the event Parcells wished to coach a team other than the Patriots in 1997, the Pats were entitled to some sort of compensation. The source was widely believed to be Bob Kraft himself. Who else could it have been?

One of the salient items in the McDonough story was the following paragraph: "However, Fraley maintained that there is no provision in the contract that would call for any type of compensation and that his client is free to do whatever he wants in '97."

That sure isn't what Kraft was saying a week earlier. The battle lines were now drawn. Other teams go to the Super Bowl and the talk is about football. Only the Patriots would go to the Super Bowl and make some 3,000 members of the international media witness to a family spat.

There would, of course, be denials all around. Parcells, when confronted with the story, went into a shameless Mickey The Dunce routine, turning each question into a battle of semantics. (eg. "What Will McDonough story? Will McDonough writes a lot of stories.") Kraft kept insisting the talk should be on the game and not on the future job status of a coach he had labeled in the immediate aftermath of the AFC title game as "the greatest coach — in modern times."

The Patriots players were now caught squarely in the middle. The attention had been successfully diverted from them and onto the coach. "The timing of it is awful," said Chris Slade, who had certainly had his difficulties with The Tuna during the course of the season. "But if you let yourself get caught up in it...there will always be distractions, whether it's the coach, the players, a bad hotel — and you've just got to put that aside and comment after the game."

The Tuna tried to put out the fire — as you might expect. "It won't affect my team," he growled. "That's not the issue here. The issue is the New England Patriots against the Green Bay Packers in Super Bowl XXXI."

Not any more, it wasn't. The owner was forced to weigh in, of course. "To me, it's unfortunate that Mr. Fraley took this time to try to put something in the paper, and I don't think the fans in New England want to concentrate on this right now," said Kraft.

Back home, many people were livid. They could not understand how a local paper would print such a potentially distracting and clearly controversial story at that juncture. Many people still believe that the role of the sports section is to cheerlead for the local teams, rather than report on them.

The artistic low point came on the morning of Wednesday, January 22. The two men with large egos revealed themselves to be men of limited common sense. Somehow thinking that they could bring smiles to the faces of the assembled media by making light of their differences, they collaborated in as embarrassing a scene as there has ever been at a Super Bowl.

Parcells spoke first. He sounded serious enough. "...You know, there's been a little bit, kind of swirling around here, so my final statement is the same as it has been — Bob and I agreed a long time ago that we would go through this year and we would discuss the situation about the future when the season is over...and we're gonna do that as expeditiously as possible, and I can also assure you that it's going to be done in a very friendly and civil manner...Bob has a little something to say to you."

Nothing wrong with that, correct? But it turned to be a straight man line. Bob Kraft took the microphone and proceeded to make a 100 percent fool of himself. He'll never again lack for atonement thoughts on Yom Kippur.

"Thank you very much, Bill," he began. "I'm glad you set me up this way, because we negotiated all night (gasps from the audience) and I'm happy to announce that Bill Parcells will be the new manager, he signed a 10-year contract to be the new manager of our paper and packaging group, Rand-Whitney and International Paper Products. And because you know he manages money so well, he will also be the chief executive of our Chestnut Hill Management."

There was more, but you get the point. No, it was no funnier to have been there than it is to read it on paper.

"Which one was the dog and which one was the pony?" inquired one scribe.

Kraft's explanation: "Yesterday, when we were chatting, and it seemed to get a little intense, so people thought we didn't have a good time together, he said, 'Come on. Why don't you join me at my press conference tomorrow?' We've had fun together. I don't think we've ever had a real serious argument with him in all the time he's been here. It's basically an agent and/or media topic."

Oh.

Meanwhile, those with both broader and longer memories were making great use of the trusty phrase, *deja vu*. People in Boston had forgotten that Parcells had greatly upset the Giants' front office and management during each of his previous visits to the Super Bowl. He had flirted with the Atlanta Falcons back in 1987, eventually being forced back to honor his Giants' contract by commissioner Pete Rozelle. Four years later he was batting his eyelashes at Tampa Bay in a similar scenario.

"He did it in '87 and he was playing footsie with Tampa Bay in '91," smirked one veteran, knowledgeable NFL observer. "He's not going to address this. He lies to his (supposed) buddies in the media all the time. They suck up to him, and he still lies to them. He's just a congenital liar."

Giants general manager George Young summed it all up. "Why can't he just allow an owner to enjoy a Super Bowl in peace?" he inquired.

The Parcells/Kraft hijinks aside, for everyone outside New England this game was all about a Green Bay coronation. Just about every writer and broadcaster in America had already made two pilgrimages, the first to Green Bay for the obligatory story about the team's community ownership and fanatical devotion to the cause, and the second to Kiln, Mississippi, home town of Green Bay's ebullient, and quite skillful, quarterback, Brett Favre. In fact, if you were to stop the average American football fan and ask who was playing in Super Bowl XXXI, the normal response would have been, "The Green Bay Packers vs. The Whatchamacallits."

Parcells was getting a lot of attention, not only for the question as to what he would do next, but also simply because he was Bill Parcells, a two-time Super Bowl winner. But he made it clear he didn't think there was going to be any coaching advantage for the Patriots because he had the utmost respect for Green Bay coach Mike Holmgren. But the Packers were able to use the disproportionate amount of ink spilled on the Patriots' coach, as opposed to their very competent, but lesser-known coach, to their psychological advantage.

It was now very clear that this was going to be Bill Parcells' final game as a Patriots/Whatchamacallits coach. It was time for some reflection. He was asked why he had come to the Patriots four years earlier, given that the situation looked so helpless and the history of the organization was so forbidding.

"I didn't look at it that way," he explained. "The way I looked at it, here was a coaching job. I had been there before (as an assistant in 1980). I knew some of the people who were still with the organization. I knew my way around. That represented a little bit of a comfort zone.

"And we had the number one pick," he continued. "That allowed us to get Drew Bledsoe and put a key piece of the puzzle in place."

He seized the occasion to assess the 1996 Patriots. "This is a very unified, determined, spunky, high-grade, quality-person team," he said. "There have been no (discipline) problems. They've been fun to coach. The team has continually responded to coaching and direction. It's not a hard team to coach; it's easy."

And now the unified, determined, spunky, high-grade, quality-person AFC champion New England Patriots were about to play the biggest game of their lives. They were about to go up against the heavily favored Green Bay Packers in Super Bowl XXXI.

The Patriots and Packers meet on the carpet of the New Orleans Superdome in Super Bowl XXXI. (Photo©Tom Miller)

The Super Bowl

January 26 at New Orleans

Green Bay 35, New England 21

The Las Vegas wise guys knew what they were talking about all along. They said the Packers would win by 14, and they won by 14. Good for them, but it wasn't that simple.

There had been a great deal of pregame talk about the importance of Big Plays. Each team had Big Play capability. The Packers had broken numerous Big Plays all season long. Desmond Howard had returned five kicks of varying descriptions for touchdowns. Favre was always a threat to bust a big play. The Patriots? Ask the Steelers. They'll fill you in.

The Big Play talk turned out to have a great deal of validity. Big Plays made champions out of the Green Bay Packers in Super Bowl XXXI. There was a startling 54-yard touchdown pass from Favre to Andre Rison on the second

Green Bay play from scrimmage. There was a jolting 81-yard touchdown pass from Favre to Antonio Freeman at the outset of the second quarter. And there was the crusher, an electrifying 99-yard kickoff return by the menacing Desmond Howard early in the fourth quarter.

The Howard return was a thorough boot in the Patriots' posterior, because it came in response to an 18-yard run by Curtis Martin that had brought the Pats within six points at 27-21 seventeen seconds earlier. The Patriots appeared to have found their offense again midway through the third period, but while they were busily congratulating themselves, Howard was even busier, making himself the first return specialist to be named as the Most Valuable Player in a Super Bowl.

"That kick return provided tremendous impetus for their team," said Parcells. "I thought we might have had them rocking a little bit at 27-21. We had momentum on our drive, and our defense was playing better, but he made the big play."

Most Super Bowls, particularly those of recent vintage, aren't usually very good football games, for the simple reason that the AFC team generally can't match the NFC team. This was a good football game. The Patriots did not pull a repeat of 1986.

They got down quickly by a 10-0 score, but by the end of the first period they were ahead, 14-10, and the place was abuzz. The first touchdown came at the end of a 79-yard drive, the highlights of which were a 32-yard pass from Bledsoe to Keith Byars and a 20-yard Bledsoe aerial to Martin. Throw in a Craig Newsome end zone pass interference penalty, and Bledsoe was in position to hit Byars with a one-yard TD pass.

The Patriots took the lead on a four-yard TD pass from Bledsoe to Ben Coates. The big play in this drive was a 44-yard toss to Glenn, who didn't seem to have any

Drew Bledsoe prepares to take a snap as the Patriots met the Packers in Super Bowl XXXI. (Photo©James W. Beiver)

more problems operating against the vaunted Packers as he did against the hapless Jets.

Bledsoe was the beneficiary of a sound game plan. He was able to keep the Packers off-balance with nice play-action fakes and crisp short passes, such as the one he threw to spring Byars for the 32-yarder in the first touchdown drive. Long forgotten were those horrible Steve Sax bouncers of the early season. It had been a couple of months since any intended receiver had found it necessary to make one of those "American League Player of the Week" receptions in order to latch onto a five-yard pass.

Favre had a very well-earned reputation for starting slowly and for heaving his first few passes over his receivers' heads. Holmgren referred to these uncatchable tosses as "rocket balls." But there were no "rocket balls" in his repertoire in this game.

"I said during the week ,'Who knows, I may start out on fire?'" he said. "So I did."

Green Bay took the lead back on that 81-yarder to Freeman, who made Favre look good on an audible by blowing by Lawyer Milloy. They would never trail again.

A Favre madcap dive at the flag made it 27-14 early in the third. But the Patriots came right back, taking advantage of some Holmgren substitutions in his defensive line. Bledsoe took the team from its own 47 to the Green Bay 18, whereupon Martin finished things off with an 18-yard blast right up the gut. Martin would finish with 42 yards in a mere 11 carries, thereby prompting one of the many intriguing postgame queries which would follow Parcells and staff out of town.

To this point the Patriots had contained Mr. Howard, at least on kickoffs. He was proving to be a difficult customer on punt returns — finishing with six for 90 yards — but kickoffs were another matter. Until now.

It was easy for people after the fact to say, "Why kick to Desmond Howard?" But the Patriots had been executing their schemes successfully, so why not? This time Howard made them pay, taking the kickoff and heading straight upfield. Marty Moore had a brief shot at him. Hasan Graham had another brief chance and Vinatieri had an even briefer look. That was all, Bye-bye.

"Desmond Howard ruined a perfectly good game," sighed defensive coordinator Al Groh. "He put Bourbon Street in a different perspective. After that, it didn't seem like such a fun place."

One of the great postgame what-ifs? concerned Hasan Graham. He was playing in place of the reliable, irreplaceable Troy Brown, who was scratched just prior to the game for an injury of some sort. Let's call that a mystery injury of some sort, because not once all week did Parcells or anyone else in authority hint that there

Bruce Armstrong (78) helps to clear a path for Curtis Martin. Martin finished the game with 42 yards on 11 carries, including an 18-yard touchdown run. (Photo©James W. Biever)

Bledsoe was 25-for-48 for 256 yards and two touchdowns — but he also threw four interceptions. (Photo©James W. Biever)

was anything wrong with Troy Brown. Whatever was ailing him, the fact is that Howard ran right by the spot that would normally have been occupied by Brown. Graham is no stiff, but he's not Troy Brown. "I found out I was playing right when I got here," he admitted.

Vinatieri had an interesting twist. "Write this down," he said. "I was coming up to get him, but I was held." Remember Herschel Walker? Vinatieri isn't just another "wimpy kicker."

"Go back and check the film and tell me I was wrong," he insisted. "Because if I didn't get held, I'll give you all the money I own."

If that be the case, there simply was no justice. And there would be no further life in the New England Patriots, either. Much would be made of two fourth-quarter sacks by Reggie White, but the Patriots more than likely weren't going anywhere. They needed two scores, and they weren't going to get them, period.

No matter how anyone wished to slice it, Green Bay had proven itself to be the better team. Favre showed why he was a two-time NFL MVP with 14 completions, good for 246 yards and two touchdowns. He threw no interceptions.

The Packers balanced off a strong passing game with 115 yards on the ground. The defense did what it had to do. And then there was Desmond Howard...

Drew Bledsoe, who, aside from an occasional wonderful pass here and there did not have an especially great playoffs, finished his season with 25 completions in 48 attempts. He racked up 256 yards. He threw two touchdown passes, but he was intercepted four times. He was OK. But he is not Brett Favre — yet.

To him, the major item of postgame discussion should have been Big Plays. "That's the bottom line in this game," he said. "You watch, year in and year out. Super Bowls are won on big plays. The Packers made more big plays than we did. They didn't turn the ball over and they basically played mistake-free football. They played a very good game today and we weren't able to play at that level."

Postscript

Events unfolded quickly after Super Bowl XXXI.

Bill Parcells and Bob Kraft wound up communicating via attorneys. Parcells and his legal beagles contended that he was contractually free to coach wherever he chose in 1997 because he had fulfilled the necessary provisions to extricate himself cleanly. Kraft and his legal beagles contended that Parcells could only coach elsewhere in 1997 with the express permission of Bob Kraft.

The matter was referred to commissioner Paul Tagliabue, himself an attorney. He ran it by his own well-paid legal beagles and the decision was swift.

The headline of the January 30 *Boston Globe*:

Kraft Wins Sticking Point

Kraft's viewpoint had been upheld.

That was a Thursday, a mere four days after the Super Bowl. The next day Parcells and Kraft held back-to-back press conferences. The Tuna's was to say good-bye. He was thoroughly disingenuous. He said his differences with Bob Kraft were "not about power." He talked of "philosophical differences," but declined to specify.

Amazingly, he maintained that during the more than three years he had been in Kraft's employ he had never once had an opportunity to sit down with the man signing his ample paychecks (each annual salary in excess of $1 million) for a heart-to-heart talk which might lead to ironing out those "philosophical differences."

He also said he had no idea what he would be doing in 1997. Quoting lovable Sgt. Schultz from *Hogan's Heroes*, he smiled and said, "I know nothing."

He did allude to the draft day problems. "If they want you to cook the dinner," he said, "at least they ought to let you shop for some of the groceries." Ha-ha. The fact is that he had always been able to shop for *some* of the groceries. He just wasn't being allowed to shop for *all* of the groceries. Kraft had wearied of throwing bad money at too many dubious free agent signings. After a while, he had decided that Parcells was a better coach than personnel man. That's no disgrace, but The Tuna didn't agree.

One reason Kraft had stripped Parcells of his all-encompassing Final Say was that he figured he and his family would still be owning the team long after Parcells had moved on. Is this an illogical thought process? Most people would say no.

Parcells was gone. Almost immediately, Kraft announced the appointment of former San Francisco defensive coordinator Pete Carroll as his new head coach. Carroll had signed a five-year contract. Carroll had no burning desire to shop for all the groceries.

The following Tuesday, the New York Jets made an announcement. Bill Parcells had just agreed to a long-term contract. He would be a "consultant" in 1997. Bill Belichick would be head coach. Parcells would take over in 1998, for at least four years. When he decided to step down, Belichick would again take over the team.

The Patriots protested. The commissioner had stated that Bill Parcells could neither hold the job of head coach, general manager or any "comparable position." The consultancy was, according to Kraft, a "transparent farce." After much harrumphing on both sides, the matter landed back in the lap of the commissioner. Kraft was demanding the Jets' 1997 pick, which just happened to be the number one pick in the draft. Parcells and the Jets said absolutely no way. The Tuna had his eye on University of Tennessee quarterback Peyton Manning, who, assuming he would decide to make himself eligible for the draft, had a shot at being the Drew Bledsoe of 1997.

On Monday, February 10, Kraft and Jets owner Leon Hess went to New York to see Paul Tagliabue. At 3:30 in the afternoon, with nothing resolved, Tagliabue asked the two if they would accede to a binding arbitration. He, the commissioner, would make a compensation decision. They both agreed.

At 5 p.m. Tagliabue made his decision. The Jets could have Bill Parcells' immediate services as coach. In exchange, the Patriots would receive the Jets' fourth-round pick in 1997, their second- and third-round picks in 1998 and their first-round pick in 1999. In addition, the Jets would contribute $300,000 to the Patriots' Charities.

The Parcells Era was now officially over. He could have, and should have, gone out with more grace, but he had kept a promise made the day he signed on as coach. "I said when I came to New England that I would not rest until this team could compete for the championship — and we've done that."

Even Bob Kraft could find no fault with that statement.